Welcome!
to Georgia Social Studies

Dear Georgia Student,

What does it take to be a hero? Our country has had many heroes who were bold and brave. This year you will read about them.

You will find out what their days were like. How did they travel? What did they eat? Were their lives like yours today?

This year you will learn these things and so much more. Your book shows your learning goals on the next pages.

It will be a big year.

You are on your way!

GEORGIA

Georgia Performance Standards

Grade 1

Historical Understandings

SS1H1 **The student will read about and describe the life of historical figures in American history.**

    a. Identify the contributions made by these figures: Benjamin Franklin (inventor/author/statesman), Thomas Jefferson (Declaration of Independence), Meriwether Lewis & William Clark with Sacagawea (exploration), Harriet Tubman (Underground Railroad), Theodore Roosevelt (National Parks and the environment), George Washington Carver (science).

    b. Describe how *everyday* life of these historical figures is similar to and different from everyday life in the present (food, clothing, homes, transportation, communication, recreation).

SS1H2 **The student will read or listen to American folktales and explain how they characterize our national heritage. The study will include John Henry, Johnny Appleseed, Davy Crockett, Paul Bunyan, and Annie Oakley.**

Geographic Understandings

SS1G1 The student will describe the cultural and geographic systems associated with the historical figures in SS1H1a.

SS1G2 The student will identify and locate his/her city, county, state, nation, and continent on a simple map or a globe.

SS1G3 The student will locate major *topographical features* of the earth's surface.

   a. Locate all of the *continents:* North America, South America, Africa, Europe, Asia, Antarctica, and Australia.

   b. Locate the major *oceans:* Arctic, Atlantic, Pacific, and Indian.

   c. Identify and describe *landforms* (mountains, deserts, valleys, plains, plateaus, and coasts).

nt/Civic Understandings

...udent will describe how the historic

...es in SS1H1a display positive character

...s of fairness, respect for others,

...ect for the environment, conservation, courage, equality, tolerance, perseverance, commitment.

SS1CG2 The student will explain the meaning of the patriotic words to *America* (My Country 'Tis of Thee) and *America the Beautiful*.

Economic Understandings

SS1E1 The student will identify *goods* that people make and *services* that people provide for each other.

SS1E2 The student will explain that people have to make *choices* about *goods* and *services* because of *scarcity*.

SS1E3 The student will describe how people are both *producers* and *consumers*.

SS1E4 The student will describe the *costs* and *benefits* of personal *spending* and *saving* choices.

HOUGHTON MIFFLIN
SOCIAL STUDIES

★ OUR COUNTRY ★

Visit **Education Place®**
www.eduplace.com/kids

HOUGHTON MIFFLIN   BOSTON

GEORGIA

★ AUTHORS ★

Senior Author
Dr. Herman J. Viola
Curator Emeritus
Smithsonian Institution

Dr. Cheryl Jennings
Project Director
Florida Institute of
 Education
University of North
 Florida

Dr. Sarah Witham
Bednarz
Associate Professor,
 Geography
Texas A&M University

Dr. Mark C. Schug
Professor and Director
Center for Economic
 Education
University of Wisconsin,
 Milwaukee

Dr. Carlos E. Cortés
Professor Emeritus, History
University of California,
Riverside

Dr. Charles S. White
Associate Professor
School of Education
Boston University

Georgia Program Consultant
Glen Blankenship

Consulting Authors

Dr. Dolores Beltran
Assistant Professor
Curriculum Instruction
California State University, Los Angeles
(Support for English Language Learners)

Dr. MaryEllen Vogt
Co-Director
California State University Center
for the Advancement of Reading
(Reading in the Content Area)

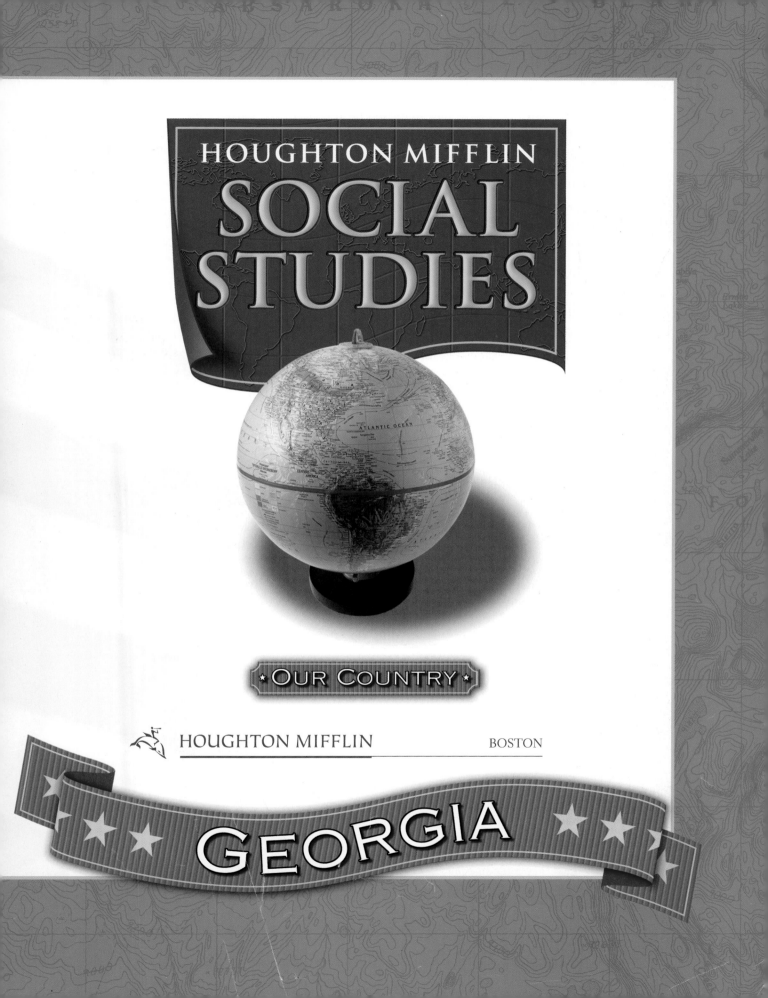

HOUGHTON MIFFLIN
SOCIAL STUDIES

★ OUR COUNTRY ★

HOUGHTON MIFFLIN   BOSTON

GEORGIA

Consultants

Philip J. Deloria
Associate Professor
Department of History
    and Program in
    American Studies
University of Michigan

Lucien Ellington
UC Professor of Education
    and Asia Program
    Co-Director
University of Tennessee,
Chattanooga

Thelma Wills Foote
Associate Professor
University of California,
Irvine

Stephen J. Fugita
Distinguished Professor
Psychology and Ethnic
    Studies
Santa Clara University

Charles C. Haynes
Senior Scholar
First Amendment Center

Ted Hemmingway
Professor of History
The Florida Agricultural &
    Mechanical University

Douglas Monroy
Professor of History
The Colorado College

Lynette K. Oshima
Assistant Professor
Department of Language,
    Literacy and Sociocultural
    Studies and Social Studies
    Program Coordinator
University of New Mexico

Jeffrey Strickland
Assistant Professor, History
University of Texas Pan
    American

Clifford E. Trafzer
Professor of History and
    American Indian Studies
University of California,
Riverside

Georgia Program Consultant

Glen Blankenship

Teacher Reviewers

Crystal Albrecht
John Sinnott Elementary
Fremont, CA

Charlene Cook
Belair Elementary
Jefferson City, MO

Katherine Donaldson
Benning Hills Elementary
Columbus, GA

Judy Jolly
Highland School
Stillman Valley, IL

Barbara Lang
Whitman Elementary
Tacoma, WA

Kay Lewis
Dalton Elementary
Aurora, CO

Anne Luckey
Oconee County
    Primary School
Watkinsville, GA

Bridget Mullet
Cobb County School District
Cobb County, GA

Mary Ann Preen
Seventh Avenue Elementary
Hadden Heights, NJ

Kerri Seid
Sequoia Elementary
Sacramento, CA

Brooke Shepard
Allen Elementary
Columbus, GA

Elizabeth Simon
Griffin Elementary
Cooper City, FL

Printed in the U.S.A.
ISBN: 13 978-0-618-49785-0
ISBN: 10 0-618-49785-4

23456789-DW-13 12 11 10 09 08 07 06

Contents

Introduction

Bringing the world to your classroom!

UNIT 1 Where We Live

26

Vocabulary Preview
Reading Strategies: Predict and Infer, Summarize

N
NW   NE
W   E
SW   SE
S

6

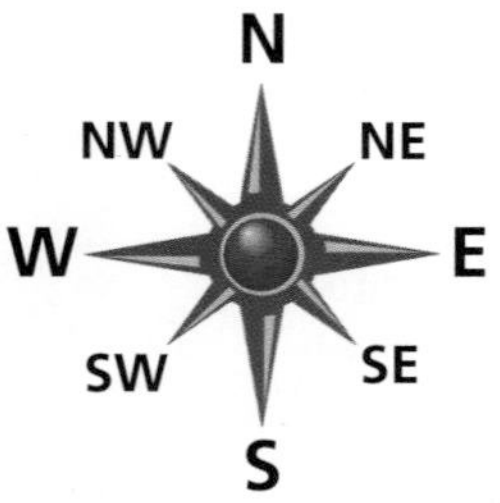

7

Vocabulary Preview
Reading Strategies: Question, Predict and Infer 154

──────────────────────── ★ ────────────────────────

American Folktales

References

Citizenship Handbook

Extend Lessons

Connect the core lesson to an important concept and dig into it. Extend your social studies knowledge!

Skill Lessons

Take a step-by-step approach to learning and practicing key social studies skills.

Visual Learning

Maps, graphs, and charts help you learn.

Maps

Timelines

Charts and Graphs

Fine Art

Primary Sources

About Your Textbook

❶ How It's Organized

Units The major sections of your book are units.
Each starts with a big idea.

Explore big ideas in geography, history, economics, government, and culture.

UNIT **1**

Where We Live

"Look about you. Take hold of the things that are here."
—George Washington Carver

The Big Idea

What do you know about Earth and its people?

26 • Unit 1   27

Get ready for reading.

Unit **3** Heroes Change America

Reading Strategy
Monitor and Clarify Use the monitor and clarify strategy in Lessons 1 and 2.
Summarize Use the summarize strategy in Lessons 3 and 4.

Each unit opens with a vocabulary preview.

● **Vocabulary Preview**

Technology
e = glossary
e = word games
www.eduplace.com/kids/hmss/

Four important concepts get you started.

history
History is the story of people and things from the past. page 115

settler
A **settler** is someone who comes to live in a new place. page 123

transportation
Transportation is a way to move people and things from place to place. A train is one kind of transportation. page 134

communication
Communication is a way people share news and ideas. A phone call is one kind of communication. page 142

112 • Unit 3   113

❷ Core and Extend

Lessons The lessons in your book have two parts: core and extend.

Core Lessons
Lessons bring social studies to life and help you meet your state's standards.

Extend Lessons
Go deeper into an important topic.

Extend
Primary Sources

Core Lesson

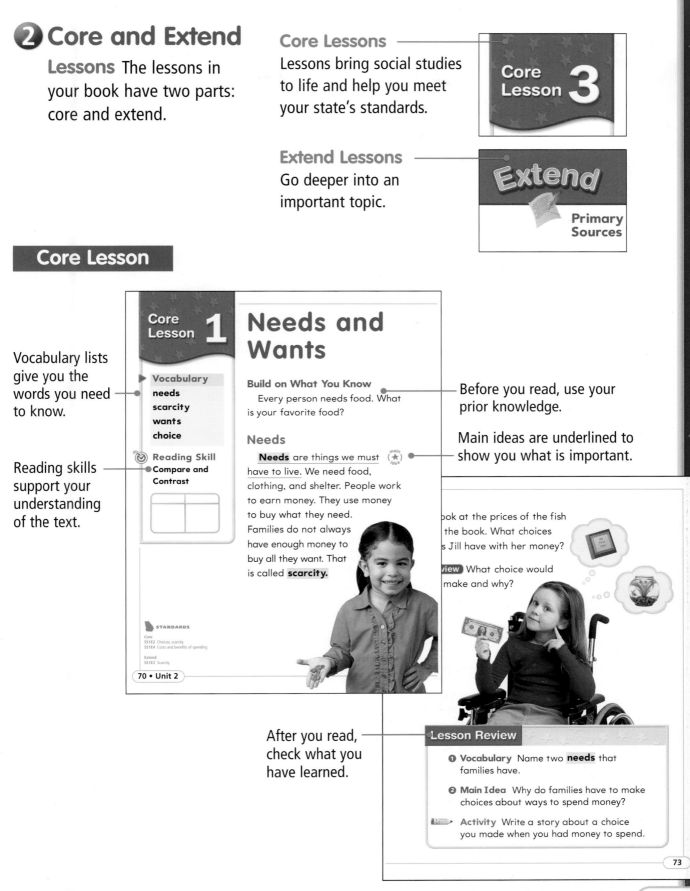

Vocabulary lists give you the words you need to know.

Reading skills support your understanding of the text.

Core Lesson 1

Needs and Wants

Vocabulary
needs
scarcity
wants
choice

Reading Skill
Compare and Contrast

Build on What You Know
Every person needs food. What is your favorite food?

Needs

Needs are things we must have to live. We need food, clothing, and shelter. People work to earn money. They use money to buy what they need. Families do not always have enough money to buy all they want. That is called **scarcity.**

STANDARDS
Core
SS1E2 Choices, scarcity
SS1E4 Costs and benefits of spending
Extend
SS1E2 Scarcity

70 • Unit 2

Before you read, use your prior knowledge.

Main ideas are underlined to show you what is important.

...ook at the prices of the fish ... the book. What choices ...s Jill have with her money?

...view) What choice would ... make and why?

After you read, check what you have learned.

Lesson Review

❶ **Vocabulary** Name two **needs** that families have.

❷ **Main Idea** Why do families have to make choices about ways to spend money?

✏ **Activity** Write a story about a choice you made when you had money to spend.

73

15

Extend Lesson Learn more about an important topic from each core lesson.

Dig in and extend your knowledge.

Extend Lesson 3
Geography

Our Georgia

Georgia has many beautiful places. Reed Bingham State Park is one. People come to fish, swim, and ride in boats. They watch birds and other animals that live safely in this park. What else might people do in a place like this?

GEORGIA
Reed Bingham
State Park

This is one of many state parks in Georgia. People can enjoy the land and the water.

Activities
1. **Think About It** Look at the picture. Tell what things are growing and what things people built.
2. **Draw It** Draw land or water that you have seen in Georgia. Write about your picture.

48 • Unit 1

49

Look for literature, readers' theater, geography, economics—and more.

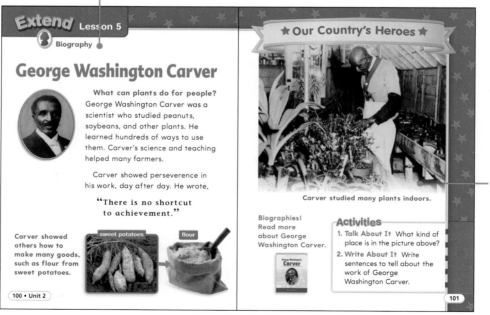

Extend Lesson 5
Biography

George Washington Carver

What can plants do for people? George Washington Carver was a scientist who studied peanuts, soybeans, and other plants. He learned hundreds of ways to use them. Carver's science and teaching helped many farmers.

Carver showed perseverence in his work, day after day. He wrote,

"There is no shortcut to achievement."

Carver showed others how to make many goods, such as flour from sweet potatoes.

sweet potatoes

flour

★ Our Country's Heroes ★

Carver studied many plants indoors.

Biographies! Read more about George Washington Carver.

George Washington Carver

Activities
1. **Talk About It** What kind of place is in the picture above?
2. **Write About It** Write sentences to tell about the work of George Washington Carver.

100 • Unit 2

101

Write, talk, draw, and role-play!

③ Skills

Skill Building Learn map, graph, and study skills, as well as citizenship skills for life.

Practice and apply each social studies skill.

Skill lessons step it out.

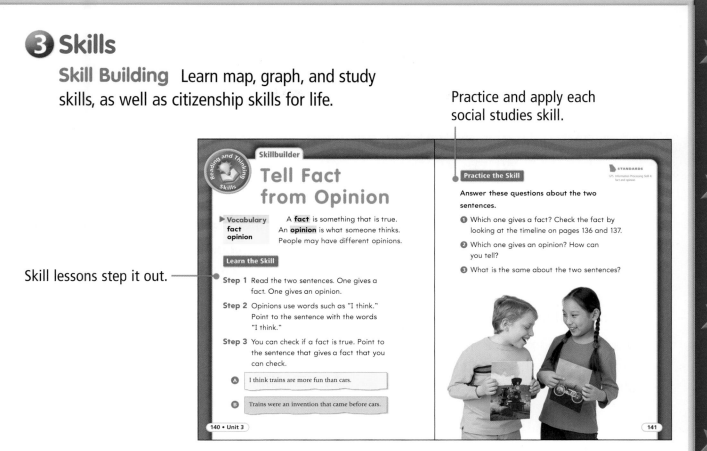

Skillbuilder

Reading and Thinking Skills

Tell Fact from Opinion

Vocabulary
fact
opinion

A **fact** is something that is true. An **opinion** is what someone thinks. People may have different opinions.

Learn the Skill

Step 1 Read the two sentences. One gives a fact. One gives an opinion.

Step 2 Opinions use words such as "I think." Point to the sentence with the words "I think."

Step 3 You can check if a fact is true. Point to the sentence that gives a fact that you can check.

Ⓐ I think trains are more fun than cars.

Ⓑ Trains were an invention that came before cars.

140 • Unit 3

Practice the Skill

STANDARDS
SS Information Processing Skill 4: fact and opinion

Answer these questions about the two sentences.

❶ Which one gives a fact? Check the fact by looking at the timeline on pages 136 and 137.

❷ Which one gives an opinion? How can you tell?

❸ What is the same about the two sentences?

141

④ References

Citizenship Handbook

The back of your book includes sections you'll refer to again and again.

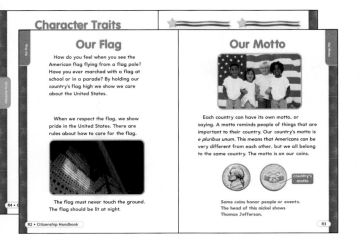

Resources

Look for atlas maps, a glossary of social studies terms, and an index.

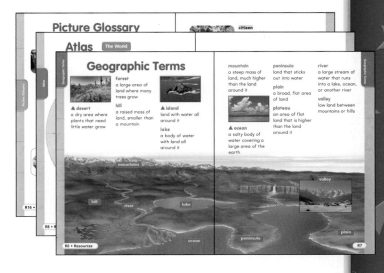

Reading Social Studies

Your book will help you be a good reader.
Here's what you will find:

VOCABULARY SUPPORT

Preview Learn four important words from the unit.

Lesson Vocabulary Learn the meanings of lesson vocabulary.

Vocabulary Practice Reuse words in the reviews, skills, and extends. Show that you know your vocabulary.

READING STRATEGIES

Look for the reading strategy at the beginning of each unit.

Predict and Infer

Monitor and Clarify

Question

Summarize

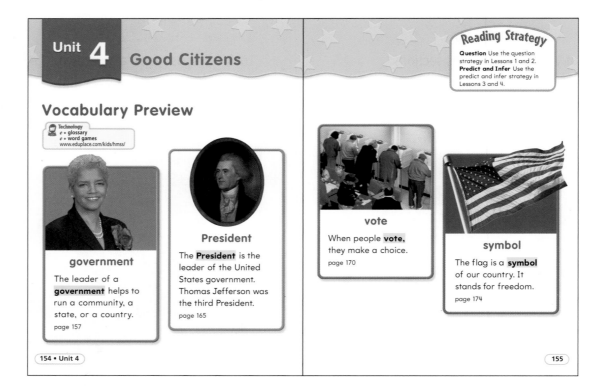

Unit **4** Good Citizens

Reading Strategy
Question Use the question strategy in Lessons 1 and 2.
Predict and Infer Use the predict and infer strategy in Lessons 3 and 4.

Vocabulary Preview

Technology
e • glossary
e • word games
www.eduplace.com/kids/hmss/

government
The leader of a **government** helps to run a community, a state, or a country.
page 157

President
The **President** is the leader of the United States government. Thomas Jefferson was the third President.
page 165

vote
When people **vote**, they make a choice.
page 170

symbol
The flag is a **symbol** of our country. It stands for freedom.
page 174

154 • Unit 4

155

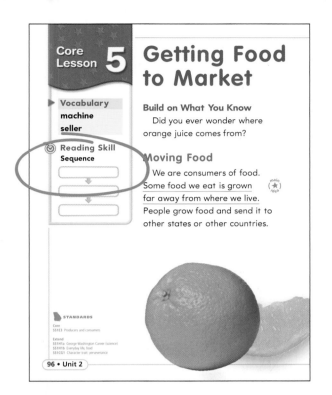

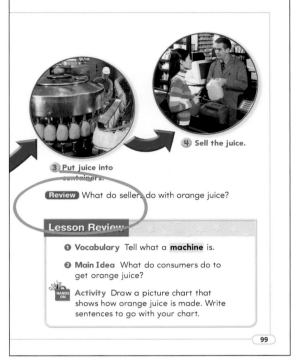

Core Lesson **5** — **Getting Food to Market**

Vocabulary
machine
seller

Reading Skill
Sequence

Build on What You Know
Did you ever wonder where orange juice comes from?

Moving Food
We are consumers of food. Some food we eat is grown far away from where we live. People grow food and send it to other states or other countries.

STANDARDS
Core
SS1E3 Producers and consumers
Extend
SS1H1a George Washington Carver (science)
SS1H1b Everyday life, food
SS1CG1 Character trait: perseverance

96 • Unit 2

3 Put juice into containers.

4 Sell the juice.

Review What do sellers do with orange juice?

Lesson Review

❶ **Vocabulary** Tell what a **machine** is.

❷ **Main Idea** What do consumers do to get orange juice?

Activity Draw a picture chart that shows how orange juice is made. Write sentences to go with your chart.

99

READING SKILLS

Graphic organizer
As you read, use the reading skills to organize the information.

Sequence

Cause and Effect

Compare and Contrast

Problem and Solution

Draw Conclusions

Predict Outcomes

Classify

Main Idea and Details

COMPREHENSION SUPPORT

Build On What You Know
Ask yourself what you know about the lesson topic. You may already know a lot!

Review Questions
Answer questions as you read. Did you understand what you read?

Social Studies
Why It Matters

Social Studies is exciting and fun. It is not just a book you read in school. You will use what you learn all your life.

WHEN I
- look around my neighborhood
- or read a map—
I'll use geography!

WHEN I
- save money or
- decide what to buy—
I'll use economics!

Town Map

WHEN I
- ► go to a neighborhood meeting
- ► or decide who to vote for—
I'll use what I've learned about citizenship!

WHEN I
- ► hear the story of a person from the past
- ► read books and visit museums
- ► look closely at the world around me—
I'll think about history!

Our Country's Heroes

We love our land, the United States of America. It is our country. We call it home. Our country has many different places and people. Heroes and everyday people are all part of the United States.

State Wildflower

The azalea is the state wildflower of Georgia.

Our Country's Heroes

Heroes are people who are brave or kind. They may show a special talent. Over time, heroes have made our country a great place to live.

Benjamin Franklin

1706–1790

His ideas helped our country change.

Thomas Jefferson

1743–1826

His words helped begin the new country.

Meriwether Lewis

1774–1809

His travels helped the country grow.

William Clark

1770–1838

His travels helped the country grow.

Biographies!
You will read about these heroes from the past.

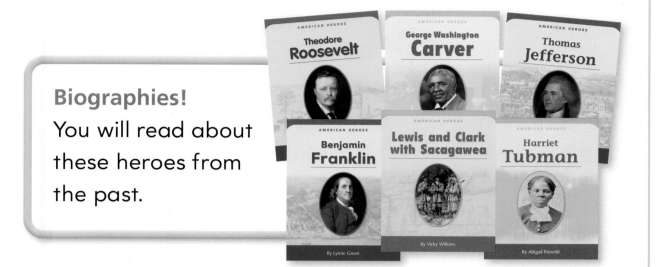

Sacagawea

1787?–1812

She led Lewis and Clark to the Pacific Ocean.

Harriet Tubman

1820?–1913

She led hundreds of people to freedom.

Theodore Roosevelt

1858–1919

This President helped save places in nature.

George Washington Carver

1864?–1943

He found many ways to use plants to improve the lives of others.

UNIT 1

Where We Live

"Look about you. Take hold of the things that are here."
—George Washington Carver

The Big Idea

What do you know about Earth and its people?

Vocabulary Preview

Technology
e • **glossary**
e • **word games**
www.eduplace.com/kids/hmss/

Continent

continent

A **continent** is a very large area of land. The continent where you live is called North America.

page 32

mountain

A **mountain** is land that is higher than all other land around it. page 44

Reading Strategy

Predict and Infer Use the predict and infer strategy in Lessons 1 and 2.
Summarize Use the summarize strategy in Lessons 3, 4, and 5.

natural resource

Water is a **natural resource** that people use every day. page 50

season

Summer is a **season** that can have hot weather. page 57

Our Earth

Build on What You Know

The world is where you live. What do you know about the world?

Earth, Our World

Earth is another name for the world where we live. It is made up of land and water. We see these on a globe. A **globe** is a model of Earth.

main idea ★

Vocabulary
globe
ocean
continent
coast

Reading Skill
Compare and Contrast

A globe shows Earth's shape. It is round like a ball.

Ocean

STANDARDS

Core
SS1G2 Locate own continent
SS1G3a Continents
SS1G3b Oceans
SS1G3 Coast

Extend
SS1G3b Pacific Ocean

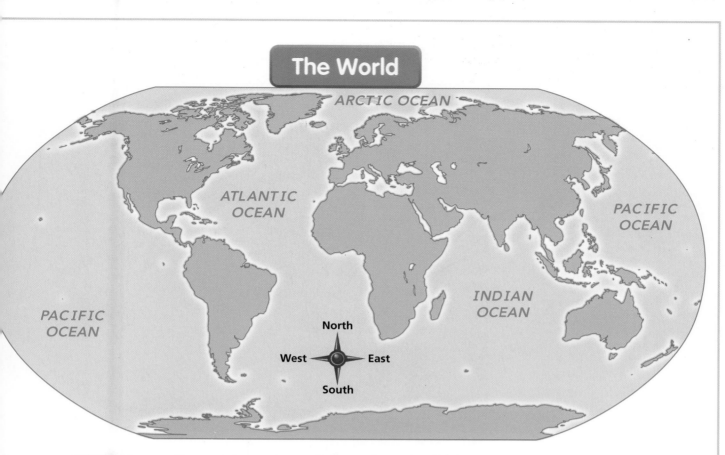

The World

ARCTIC OCEAN

ATLANTIC
OCEAN

PACIFIC
OCEAN

PACIFIC
OCEAN

INDIAN
OCEAN

North

West — East

South

Skill **Reading Maps** What does this map show?

Oceans

There is more water than land on Earth.
The large areas of water on the globe and
on the map are oceans. An **ocean** is a large
body of salty water. Earth has four oceans. (main ★ idea)

Review In what way is a globe like Earth?

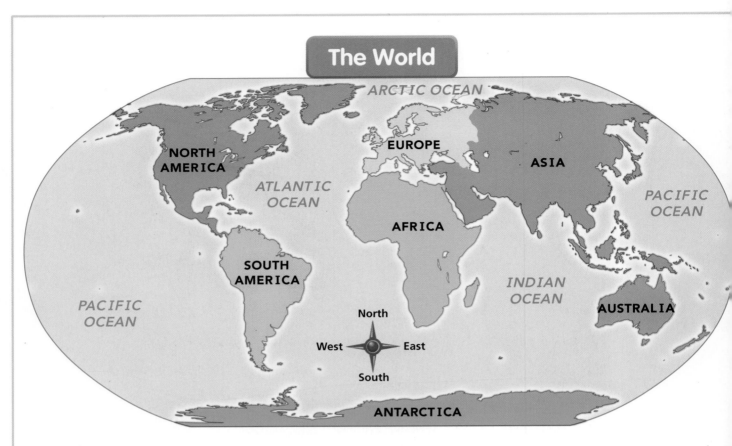

The World

ARCTIC OCEAN

NORTH AMERICA

EUROPE

ASIA

ATLANTIC OCEAN

PACIFIC OCEAN

AFRICA

SOUTH AMERICA

INDIAN OCEAN

AUSTRALIA

PACIFIC OCEAN

North

West · East

South

ANTARCTICA

Skill **Reading Maps** **What are the names of the continents?**

Continents

A very large area of land is called a **continent.** Earth has seven continents. Our country is part of the continent called North America. Find North America on the map. All continents have coasts. A **coast** is land next to the ocean.

main idea

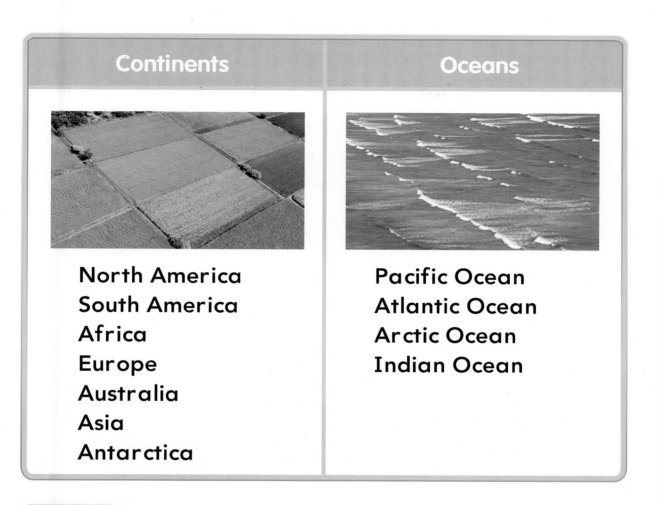

Continents	Oceans
North America South America Africa Europe Australia Asia Antarctica	Pacific Ocean Atlantic Ocean Arctic Ocean Indian Ocean

Review Name the world's oceans.

Lesson Review

❶ **Vocabulary** Tell something you know about **continents** and **oceans.**

❷ **Main Idea** What do we call the large areas of land and water on a globe?

HANDS ON **Activity** Use your finger to trace the coast of North America.

Geography

The Pacific Ocean

PACIFIC
OCEAN

Let's explore the world's biggest ocean. It touches the coasts of five continents.

There is a big colorful world of plants and animals under the ocean waves.

The ocean floor can be hilly or flat. Big volcanoes rise from deep in the Earth.

Activities

1. **Talk About It** Talk about what you see in the ocean.

2. **Create It** Cut and paste colored paper to make a picture of the ocean floor, plants, and animals.

Read a Map Key

▶ **Vocabulary**
map key
symbols

A map can show you where places are. Most maps have a map key. A **map key** helps you read the map. It helps you find places on the map.

Learn the Skill

Step 1 The places and things on a map key are shown by symbols. **Symbols** are pictures that stand for real things.

Step 2 Look at each symbol on the map key. Read the words. What real thing does each symbol stand for?

Step 3 Find a house symbol on the map. Each house symbol shows where a real house is.

Practice the Skill

Look at the map and the map key.

1 Choose a symbol on the map. Use the map key to tell what the symbol stands for.

2 Use your finger to trace a route between the school and the nearest park.

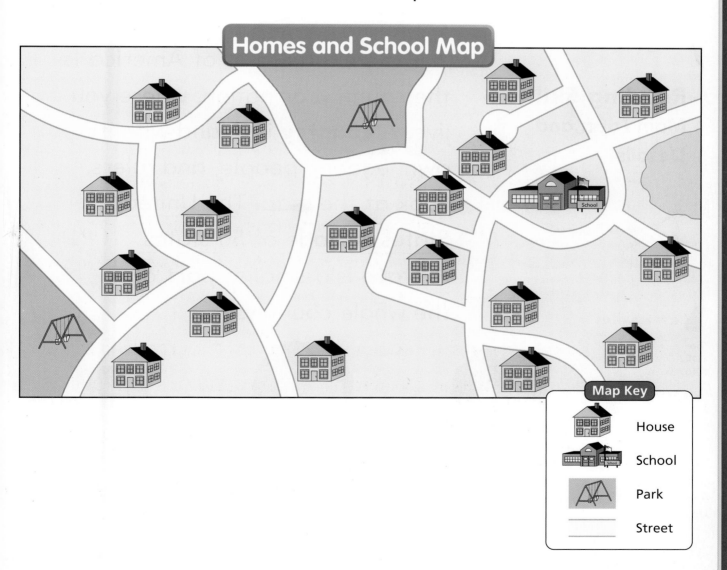

Homes and School Map

Map Key

House

School

Park

Street

Our State and Nation

Vocabulary

country

state

county

citizen

city

Reading Skill

Main Idea and Details

STANDARDS

Core
SS1G2 County, state, nation
SS1G3 Deserts

Extend
SS1CG2 America, America
the Beautiful

Build on What You Know

What do you know about the United States of America?

The United States

The United States of America is the country, or nation, where you live. A **country** is a land with its own leaders, people, and rulers. Look at the map. The United States is made of 50 states. A **state** is a smaller part of the whole country.

main idea

North

West — **East**

South

Skill **Reading Maps** Point to your
state on the map.

Citizens of Our State

Most states have many counties.
A **county** is a smaller part of a state.
Our state, Georgia, has more than
100 counties. You are a citizen of your
county, your state, and your country. A
citizen is someone who belongs to a place.

main idea

Review Which state are you a citizen of?

I LOVE GEORGIA

Places in the United States

Our country has places where many people live. Every state has some cities. A **city** is a place where many people live close to one another. Most cities have many big buildings.

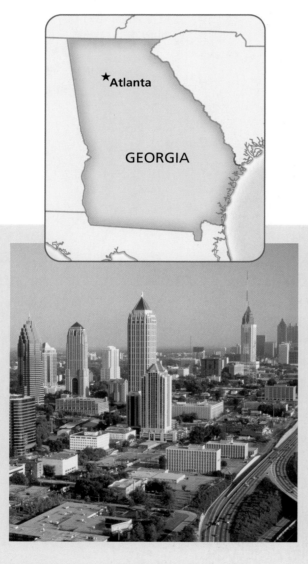

Atlanta is a city in Georgia.

New York City is in New York State.

Parts of the Sonoran Desert are in the states of Arizona and California.

Our country also has forests, farms, and deserts where few people live. A desert is a dry area of land. Every state has some places where few people live.

Review What are places where many people live?

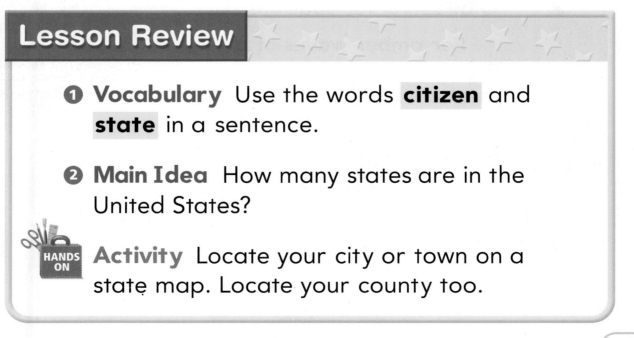

Lesson Review

❶ **Vocabulary** Use the words **citizen** and **state** in a sentence.

❷ **Main Idea** How many states are in the United States?

HANDS ON **Activity** Locate your city or town on a state map. Locate your county too.

Songs of Our Country

What can songs tell about our country?
Songs have words for the beauty we see.
They have words about the pride we feel.
Read what these two songs tell about the
land and people of America.

"America the Beautiful"

by Katharine Lee Bates

O beautiful for spacious skies,
    For amber waves of grain,
For purple mountain majesties
    Above the fruited plain.
America! America!
    God shed His grace on thee
And crown thy good with brotherhood
    From sea to shining sea.

"America"

by Samuel F. Smith

My country, 'tis of thee,

Sweet land of liberty,

   Of thee I sing;

Land where my fathers died,

Land of the Pilgrims' pride,

From every mountain-side

   Let freedom ring.

Activities

1. **Talk About It** What do you see that goes with the songs? What would you add to the picture?

2. **Sing It** Read aloud one of the songs and then sing it. What do you like about singing it?

Our Land

Vocabulary

landform
mountain
plain
valley
plateau

Reading Skill
Compare and Contrast

Build on What You Know

Think of the land around your school. Is it flat or hilly?

Kinds of Land

Deserts are one kind of land. Some other kinds of land are called landforms. **Landforms** are different shapes of land. A **mountain** is a landform that is higher than the land around it. Earth is made up of landforms. *(★) main idea*

Mt. McKinley is in Alaska.

ALASKA

STANDARDS

Core
SS1G3 Landforms and deserts

Extend
SS1G3 Landforms

A **plain** is a flat landform. Some plains are grassy. Other plains have good soil for farming. Plains can be high land or low land.

Review What are two landforms?

Nebraska has high grassy plains.

NEBRASKA

Valleys and Plateaus

Another landform is a valley. A **valley** is low land between mountains or hills. Look at the shape of the valley in the picture.

▼ Georgia has valleys. These valleys are in Black Rock Mountain State Park.

Georgia has plateaus like this one in Cloud Canyon State Park.

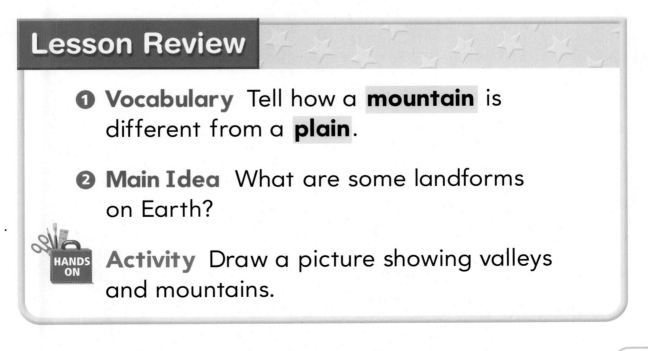

Landforms

| mountain | plain | valley | plateau |

Which is the highest landform on the chart?

A **plateau** is a landform too. A plateau is flat and higher than the land around it. Its shape is different from a mountain.

Review Compare a valley to a plateau.

Lesson Review

❶ **Vocabulary** Tell how a **mountain** is different from a **plain**.

❷ **Main Idea** What are some landforms on Earth?

Activity Draw a picture showing valleys and mountains.

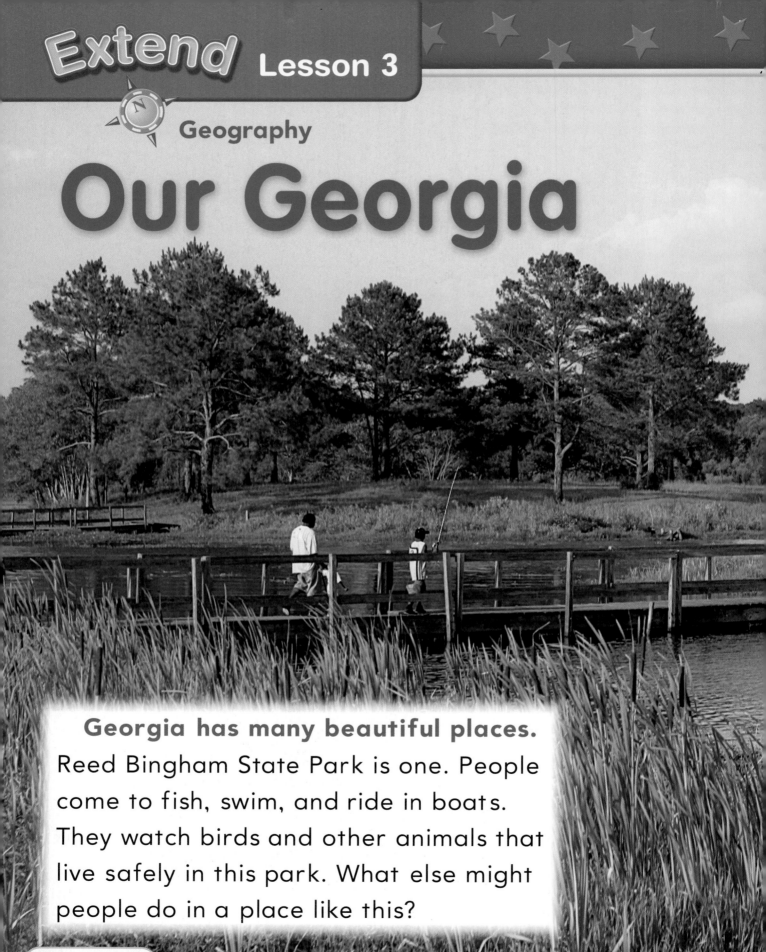

Our Georgia

Georgia has many beautiful places. Reed Bingham State Park is one. People come to fish, swim, and ride in boats. They watch birds and other animals that live safely in this park. What else might people do in a place like this?

GEORGIA

Reed Bingham
State Park

This is one of many state parks in Georgia. People can enjoy the land and the water.

Activities

1. **Think About It** Look at the picture. What things are part of nature and what things have people made?

2. **Draw It** Draw land or water that you have seen in Georgia. Write about your picture.

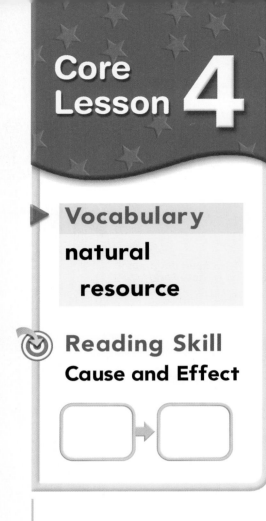
Natural Resources

Build on What You Know

People use water and wood every day in many different ways. You use wooden pencils and you drink water.

Earth Has Natural Resources

Plants, soil, and water come from nature. Earth has natural resources. A **natural resource** is something in nature that people use.

main idea

STANDARDS

Core
SS1G1 Geographic systems

Extend
SS1H1a Theodore Roosevelt and national parks
SS1H1b Everyday life of historical figures
SS1CG1 Character trait: respect for environment

Name a natural resource in each picture.

Review What things do you see in your classroom that come from wood?

People Use and Save Resources

Oil and coal are found  under the ground. People can use those natural resources to heat homes and buildings. Oil can be made into gasoline. People use gasoline in their cars.

(main idea ★)

This man is digging for coal under the ground.

These children pick up trash that could wash back into the ocean.

Many people work to save natural resources such as water. They also work to replace trees that have been cut down.

Review What can you do to save water and other natural resources?

Lesson Review

❶ **Vocabulary** Tell something you know about a **natural resource.**

❷ **Main Idea** What do people do with natural resources?

HANDS ON **Activity** Use pictures and words to make a poster that shows people working to save water.

THEODORE ROOSEVELT

When he was a boy, Theodore Roosevelt loved being out in nature. When he grew up, he helped save land for animals and plants. As President, he started many national parks. Rules for the parks keep animals and natural resources safe.

Theodore Roosevelt drew pictures of animals and plants when he was a boy.

★ Our Country's Heroes ★

President Roosevelt added land to Yosemite National Park in California.

Theodore Roosevelt

John Muir

Biographies!
Read more about
Theodore Roosevelt.

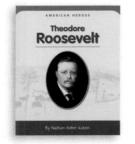

AMERICAN HEROES
Theodore
Roosevelt

By Nathan Asher Katzin

Activities

1. **Talk About It** What can you tell about Theodore Roosevelt from the picture?

2. **Draw It** Draw an animal or plant you care about. Tell what you can do to keep it safe.

Weather and Seasons

Vocabulary
weather
season

Reading Skill
Cause and Effect

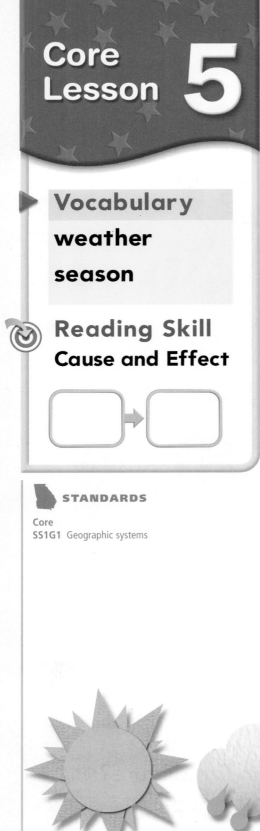

STANDARDS
Core
SS1G1 Geographic systems

Build on What You Know

Look out the window. Is it sunny or cloudy? People like sunny days for working and playing outside.

Weather

Weather is what it is like outside. Weather is always moving and changing. Winds cause the weather to change. Rain, wind, clouds, and temperature are all part of weather.

main idea

sunny   rainy   snowy   cloudy

Seasons

A **season** is a time of the year. <u>Fall, winter, spring, and summer are the four seasons.</u> Each season has different weather.

Review What season is it now?

Seasons

Spring

Summer

Fall

Winter

Dressing for the Weather

Seasons and weather change how people live. Children wear warm clothes in cold weather. They can go to the beach in hot weather. People may have to change their clothes because of weather.

In the United States, winter can be cold or hot. It depends on where you live.

Los Angeles

Temperatures on a February Day	
Miami, Florida	73°
Chicago, Illinois	30°
Los Angeles, California	65°
Atlanta, Georgia	57°

Review What is winter weather like where you live?

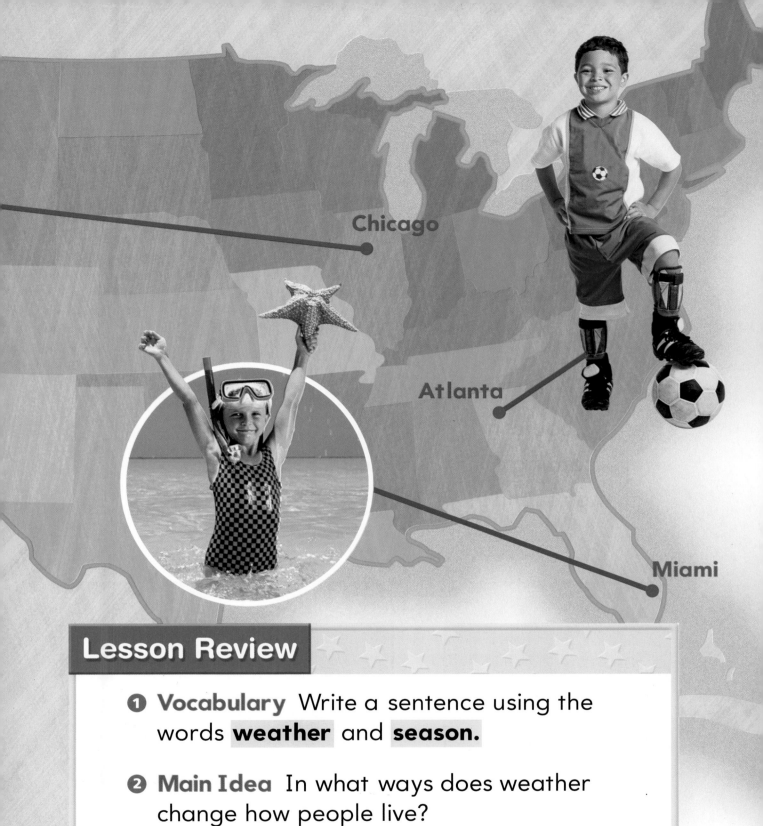

Chicago

Atlanta

Miami

Lesson Review

❶ **Vocabulary** Write a sentence using the words **weather** and **season.**

❷ **Main Idea** In what ways does weather change how people live?

HANDS ON **Activity** Make a picture book about the four seasons where you live.

What Will the Weather Be?

Then

Long ago, there were no weather reports. People could not find out if rain or snow were coming. They did have some old weather sayings.

Cows lying down
Good chance of rain

If anthills are high in July,
Winter will be stormy.

Now

Today weather reporters find out what the weather will be. They use satellites and computers. Satellites take pictures of weather across the world. The pictures show where big storms are.

Activities

1. **Compare It** Tell what you see in the pictures that go with "Then" and the picture that goes with "Now."

2. **Create It** Make a chart that shows the weather for each day of one week.

Big Idea

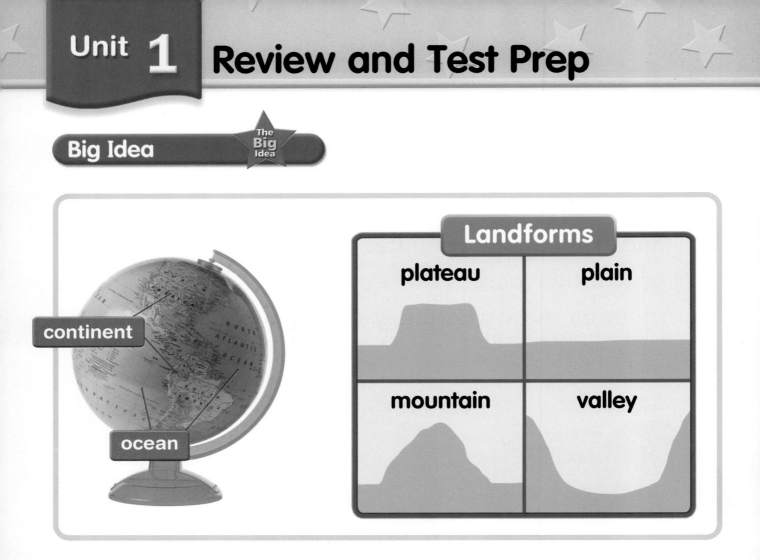

Landforms

plateau | plain

mountain | valley

continent

ocean

Use the chart and globe to help answer the questions.

1. What does a globe show? (page 30)

2. Point to and name the continent we live on. (page 32)

3. Plateaus, valleys, plains, and _____ are landforms. (page 47)

Facts and Main Ideas

4. What are the names of Earth's continents? (page 32)

5. What country is Georgia in? (page 39)

6. What are the names of Earth's oceans? (page 31)

Vocabulary

Write the letter or word for each correct answer.

7. Africa is a _____ .

8. Trees are a _____ .

9. A _____ is a time of the year.

10. An _____ is a large body of salty water.

A. season (page 57)

B. state (page 38)

C. continent (page 32)

D. ocean (page 31)

E. natural resource (page 50)

Test Practice

11. What does the word **citizen** mean?

   A. A place with many people living in it

   B. A person who belongs to a state or a country

   C. A place that is hot and wet in summer

   D. Another name for a continent

Critical Thinking

Cause and Effect

12. What did Theodore Roosevelt do to save natural resources?

13. What causes weather to change?

Review and Test Prep

Skillbuilder

Read a Map Key

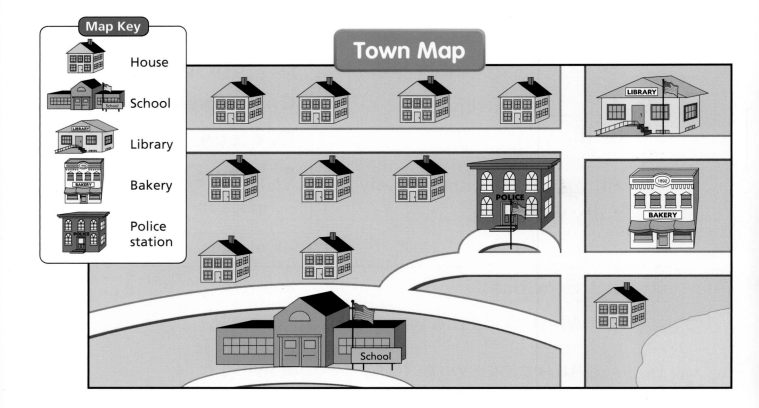

14. How many symbols are on the map key?

15. What is the same about all the symbols?

16. Which symbol is in many places on the map?

17. Name all the symbols on the town map.

Connect to Georgia

Unit Activity

Global Address Envelope

Your global address is where you live in the world.

1 Fold a big sheet of paper in half to make the envelope.

2 Write your name, street, town, county, state, country, and world.

3 Make a stamp.

Kim Lee
21 Green Street
Atlanta
Fulton County
Georgia
United States
Earth

CURRENT EVENTS
WEEKLY (WR) READER

Current Events

Make a poster of **Places in the News**. Find current events from Weekly Reader on the social studies website.

Technology

Read articles about current events at www.eduplace.com/kids/hmss/

Personal Finance

People have jobs to earn money. There are many different kinds of jobs. Name some jobs that use natural resources.

American Heroes

Read About It

Learn more about Theodore Roosevelt in his biography.

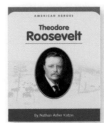

Americans at Work

> ❝Never spend your money before you have it.❞
> —Thomas Jefferson

The Big Idea

What choices do people make to get the things they want?

Vocabulary Preview

Technology
e • **glossary**
e • **word games**
www.eduplace.com/kids/hmss/

goods

Goods are things we buy or use. A supermarket sells many goods like vegetables and fruit.

page 79

services

The post office has many mail **services.**

page 79

Reading Strategy

Monitor and Clarify Use the monitor and clarify strategy in Lessons 1, 2, and 3.
Summarize Use the summarize strategy in Lessons 4 and 5.

save

Many children **save** money for things they want. page 87

factory

A **factory** is a building where workers use machines to make goods. Toys are made in a factory. page 92

Needs and Wants

Vocabulary

needs

scarcity

wants

choice

Reading Skill
Compare and Contrast

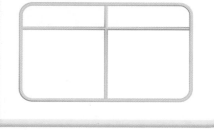

Build on What You Know

Every person needs food. What is your favorite food?

Needs

Needs are things we must have to live. We need food, clothing, and shelter. People work to earn money. They use money to buy what they need. Families do not always have enough money to buy all they want. That is called **scarcity.**

main idea (★)

 **STANDARDS**

Core
SS1E2 Choices, scarcity
SS1E4 Costs and benefits of spending

Extend
SS1E2 Scarcity

Things People Need			
Needs	North America	Africa	Asia
Shelter			
Food			
Clothing			

Review What do people do to get what they need?

Wants

Wants are things we would like to have. People make choices about how to spend money for their wants. A **choice** is what someone chooses.

Jill has one dollar saved in her bank.

She wants to get another fish for her fishbowl.

$1.00

Today she saw a book she wants.

My First Year

$2.00

Help Jill make a choice about what to buy.

Look at the prices of the fish and the book. What choices does Jill have with her money?

Review What choice would you make and why?

Lesson Review

❶ **Vocabulary** Name two **needs** that families have.

❷ **Main Idea** Why do families have to make choices about ways to spend money?

Activity Write a story about a choice you made when you had money to spend.

Stone Soup
A folktale from Europe

Once upon a time, there was a long dry spell. The people of one village didn't have much food. A young girl solved the problem of scarcity for that day's meal.

"Let's make stone soup!" said the girl. "All we need is a big pot of water and wood for a fire."

Some people brought a little water. Others brought logs for the fire.

"Here I have a stone from the river," the girl said. Plop! She dropped the stone into the pot.

The water boiled. "This smells good," the girl said. "But it would be even better with a few onions."

A few people ran home. They came back with onions for the pot.

The water boiled. "This smells just right," the girl said. "But it would be even better if we had some carrots."

More people ran home. Each one came back with a carrot or two for the pot.

The girl stirred the soup. "This soup is almost done," she said. "If we just had some noodles…"

Three or four people ran off. Soon they came back with noodles for the pot.

The soup boiled. The girl served stone soup to everyone. When they had eaten the last drop, the girl plucked the stone from the pot. She wiped it off, and put it in her pocket.

"Tomorrow," she said, "we can make stone stew!"

Activities

1. **Think About It** What is the main idea of the story?

2. **Write It** Write a recipe for stone soup.

Core Lesson 2

Goods and Services

Vocabulary

sell

goods

services

volunteer

Reading Skill
Classify

STANDARDS

Core
SS1E1 Goods and services

Extend
SS1E1 Services

Build on What You know

Think of a store where there are things to buy and people to help you. What store is it?

Making Money

People work to earn money to buy things. People also sell things to get money. To **sell** means to give things for money.

GAS
Fruit & Vegetables
HAR

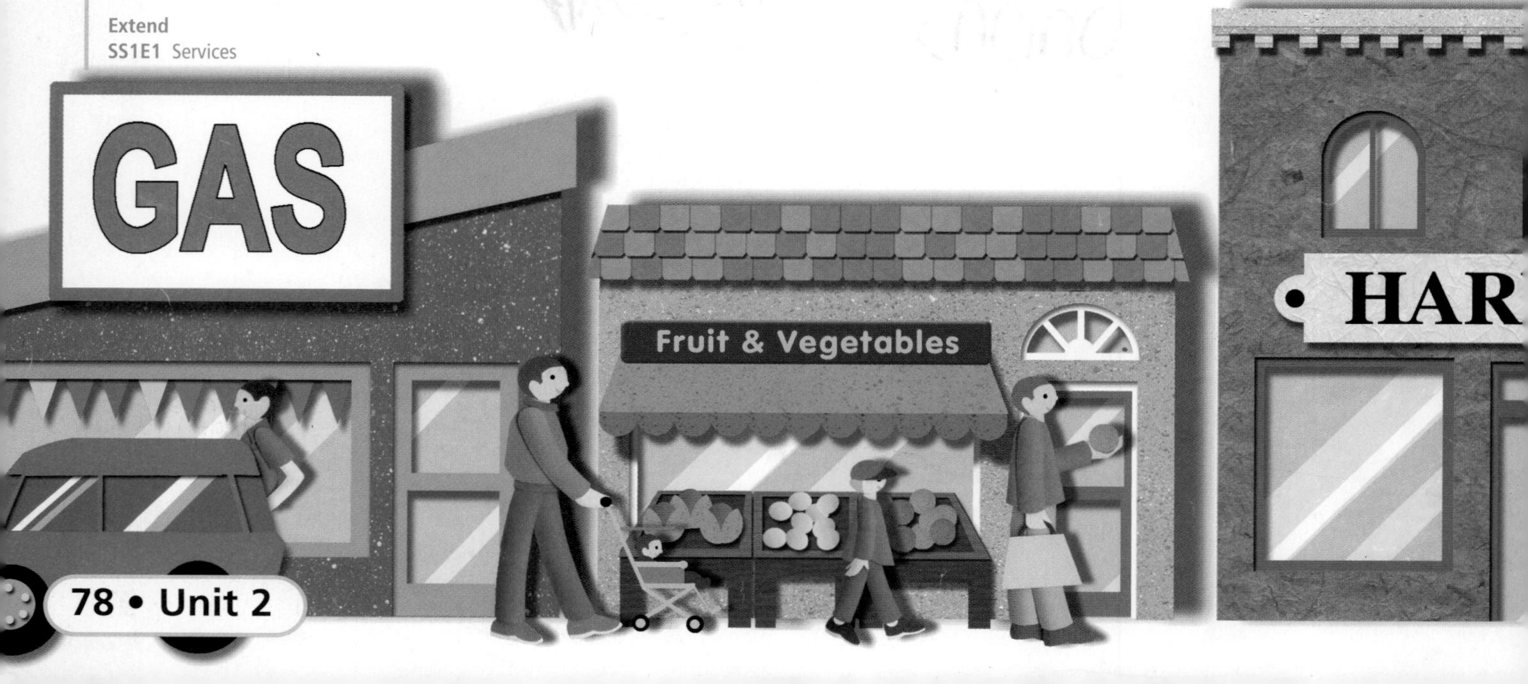

Goods and Services

Food, books, homes, cars, and shoes are goods. **Goods** are the things we buy or use. People may sell goods to make money.

A dentist and a taxi driver earn money for the services they do. **Services** are jobs people do to help others. People work to buy goods and get services. A **volunteer** is a person who helps others for no money. Can you name the goods and the services in the picture below?

main
idea

Review What are two ways people can earn money to buy things they need?

Community Goods and Services

In your city or town there are places where (★) main idea you can get goods and services. Look at the chart on this page. It shows some places where people get goods and services.

Goods	Services
Stores	Doctor's Office
Bakery	Library
Flower Shop	Hospital
Farm	Post Office
Gas Station	Town Hall
Yard Sale	Fire Station

Goods and Services Jobs

Some people have jobs making goods. Other people have service jobs. A mail carrier does a service job. Look at the children selling lemonade. Is this job selling goods or services?

Review What are places where you get goods and services?

Lesson Review

❶ **Vocabulary** Make a list of **goods** you use every day.

❷ **Main Idea** What is the difference between goods and services?

HANDS ON **Activity** Draw a picture of someone who works in a service job.

Economics

FIRE CHIEF ROSEMARY CLOUD

Chief Cloud says, "Helping people is the thing I like best."

Let's meet a leader in a great job. Rosemary Cloud is the fire chief in East Point, Georgia. Her firefighters give many services to people in East Point. They put out fires and save people. They also work to keep homes and buildings safe from fire.

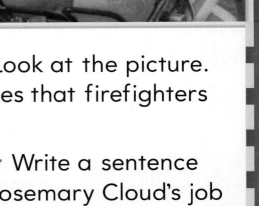

Activities

1. **Talk About It** Look at the picture. Tell some services that firefighters give people.

2. **Write About It** Write a sentence that tells why Rosemary Cloud's job is an important one.

Buy, Trade, and Save

Vocabulary

spend

cost

benefit

save

Reading Skill
Main Idea and Details

STANDARDS

Core
SS1E2 Choices
SS1E4 Costs, benefits, spending, and saving

Extend
SS1E4 Personal saving

Build on What You Know

When you want to buy something, what do you do?

Buying

When people buy things, they spend money. To **spend** means to pay. When your family shops, they look at the cost of things. The **cost** is what a person gives up, such as money. People make buying choices by looking at the cost of things they want to buy.

main idea

Trading

Sometimes people trade goods and (★) main idea services to get things they want. In school, you may like your friend's cookies and she likes your popcorn. You could trade the popcorn for the cookies.

Review Do you think it is better to buy things or trade things? Why?

I will dry the dishes for you today.

These children trade chores.

Costs and Benefits

Families have to make choices about what they can buy. Tina's parents want a bigger car because they have a new baby. Her family also wants to take a big summer vacation.

They do not have money for both. Her parents talk about the costs and benefits of each. A **benefit** is what someone hopes to get. What choice do you think they will make?

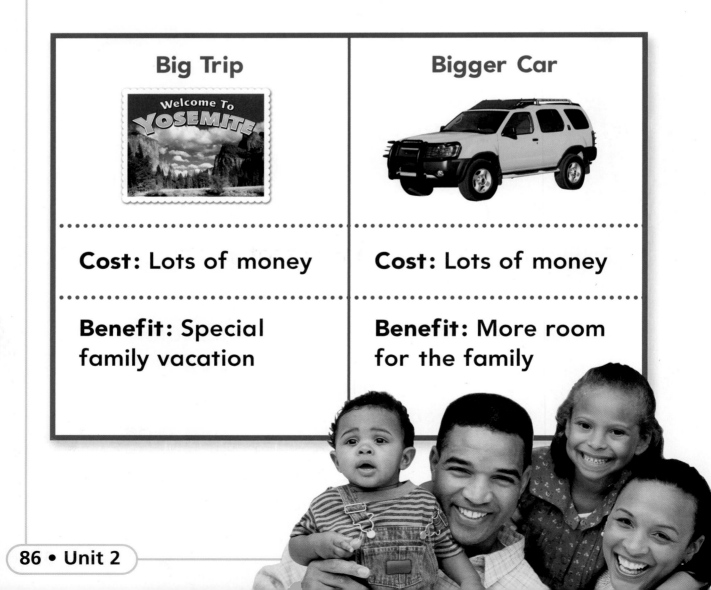

Big Trip	Bigger Car
Cost: Lots of money	**Cost:** Lots of money
Benefit: Special family vacation	**Benefit:** More room for the family

Saving Money

People often save money to buy things they want. To **save** means to put away and keep. People can save money in a bank. A benefit of saving in a bank is that your money is in a safe place.

Review What are the benefits of saving money?

Lesson Review

❶ Vocabulary Tell one way that you can **save** money.

❷ Main Idea Why do people talk about costs and benefits before they buy something?

HANDS ON **Activity** Make a shopping list of 3 things that you want to buy. Write down how much you think each thing costs.

中文

Economics

A Bank for Saving

You can save money. Make a bank and watch your money add up!

Use a plastic milk or juice container with a cap.

Step 1

Make the container into a doggy bank. Add eyes, ears, a mouth, a tail, and some feet.

Step 2

Have your teacher cut a slot for coins and bills.

Step 3

Start putting your coins in the bank today!

Producers and Consumers

Build on What You Know

What kinds of things does your family buy?

Work to Earn Money

A **consumer** is someone who buys or uses goods or services. Most adults work to earn money. They use the money to buy goods and services. People who work are producers. A **producer** is someone who makes goods or gives services. Think of the job of a producer you know.

main idea

Producers are also consumers. Mr. Cho is a mail carrier. In his job, he gives services. He is paid money to carry mail. Look at how he spent his money this week.

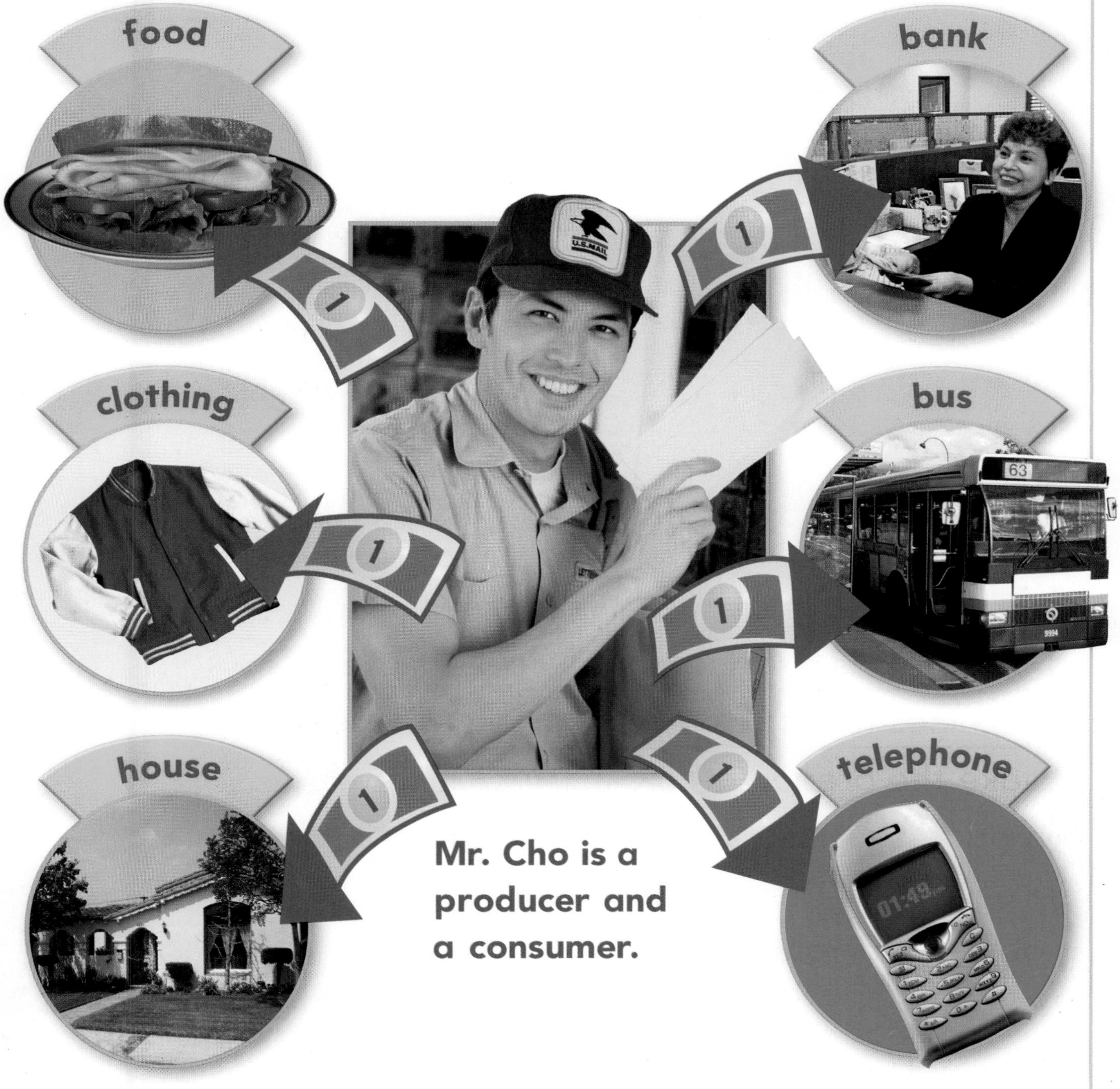
food
bank
clothing
bus
house
telephone
U.S. MAIL

Mr. Cho is a producer and a consumer.

Review What services do consumers buy?

Jobs at a Factory

This bread factory has many workers. A **factory** is a place where workers use machines to make goods. Some producers make the bread. Others put the bread in bags. Producers who work in factories are paid for their work. Everyone's job is important.

main idea

Review Who are some people who make goods?

Lesson Review

❶ **Vocabulary** Use the words **factory** and **producer** in a sentence.

❷ **Main Idea** What do people do to earn money to buy goods and services?

HANDS ON **Activity** Draw a picture of a toy factory.

Economics

Producers in the Arts

Music and dance are services for people to enjoy.

Sarah Chang

Sarah Chang was only four years old when she began to play the violin. At five years old, she was playing in concerts! Sarah Chang is now one of the best violinists in the world.

Fernando Bujones

When he was young, Fernando Bujones (Boo-hoh-nayz) was not very strong. A visit to a doctor changed his life. One day a doctor told Fernando's mother that dance lessons would make her son stronger. Fernando Bujones became a famous ballet dancer and a teacher.

Activities

1. **Talk About It** Describe the work of Sarah Chang or Fernando Bujones.

2. **Draw It** Draw a picture of a producer in music or dance. Write a sentence about your picture.

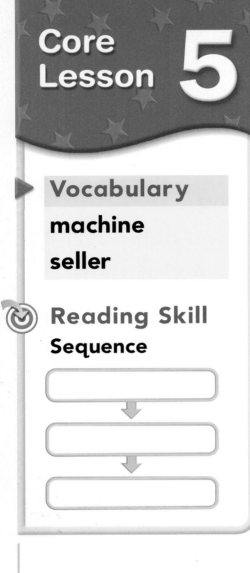

Reading Skill

Sequence

Getting Food to Market

Build on What You Know

Did you ever wonder where orange juice comes from?

Moving Food

We are consumers of food. Some food we eat is grown far away from where we live. People grow food and send it to other states or other countries.

main idea

 **STANDARDS**

Core
SS1E3 Producers and consumers

Extend
SS1H1a George Washington Carver (science)
SS1H1b Everyday life, food
SS1CG1 Character trait: perseverance

Look at the map. Orange juice in Georgia comes from California and Florida.

CALIFORNIA

GEORGIA

FLORIDA

Review Why do you think consumers want some food that is grown in other places?

From Tree to Table

It takes many workers and machines to get orange juice ready to drink. A **machine** is an object that does work for people.

When orange juice is ready, it is sent to stores. People who work at stores are sellers. A **seller** is someone who has goods and services that others can buy.

People who shop in the stores are consumers. Consumers pay money for orange juice and other goods from the stores.

1 Pick the oranges.

2 Move the oranges to the squeezing machine.

4 Sell the juice.

3 Put juice into containers.

Review What do sellers do with orange juice?

Lesson Review

1 Vocabulary Tell what a **machine** is.

2 Main Idea What do consumers do to get orange juice?

HANDS ON

Activity Draw a picture chart that shows how orange juice is made. Write sentences to go with your chart.

George Washington Carver

What can plants do for people? George Washington Carver was a scientist who studied peanuts, soybeans, and other plants. He learned hundreds of ways to use them. Carver's science and teaching helped many farmers.

Carver showed perseverance in his work, day after day. He wrote,

"There is no shortcut to achievement."

Carver showed others how to make many goods, such as flour from sweet potatoes.

sweet potatoes

flour

★ Our Country's Heroes ★

Carver studied many plants indoors.

Biographies!
Read more about George Washington Carver.

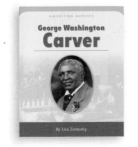

Activities

1. **Talk About It** What kind of place is in the picture above?

2. **Write About It** Write sentences to tell about the work of George Washington Carver.

Map and Globe Skills

Use a Compass Rose

▶ **Vocabulary**

compass rose

People use maps to find directions to places they go. The **compass rose** on a map shows four directions: north, south, east, and west.

Learn the Skill

Look at the globe. Put your finger on the **X** before reading each step.

Step 1 North is the direction going towards the North Pole. Move your finger north from the **X**.

Step 2 South is the direction toward the South Pole. Move your finger south from the **X**.

Step 3 When you are facing north, places to the right are east. Places to the left are west. Move your finger east and west from the **X**.

North Pole

South Pole

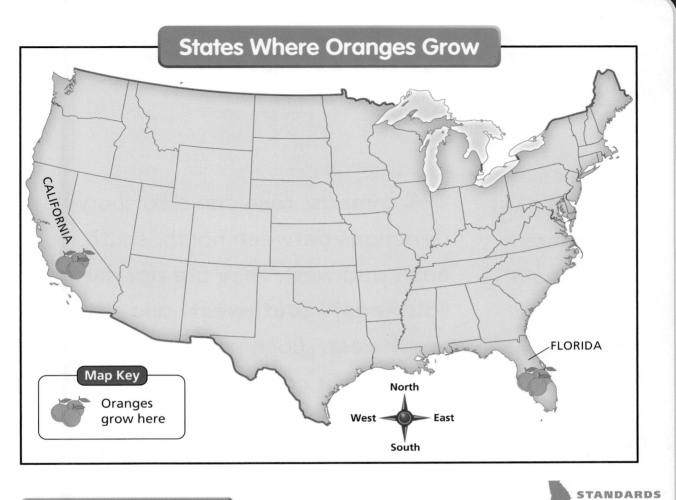

States Where Oranges Grow

CALIFORNIA

FLORIDA

Map Key

Oranges grow here

North

West — East

South

Practice the Skill

Look at the map and follow the directions.

1 Find the compass rose. Start at the oranges in Florida. Move your finger to a state north of Florida.

2 Now put your finger on California. Move your finger east across the map.

Use Intermediate Directions

▶ **Vocabulary**
northeast
southeast
southwest
northwest

A compass rose can also show the directions between north, south, east, and west. They are **northeast, southeast, southwest,** and **northwest.** Each word tells the two directions it comes between.

Learn the Skill

Look at the compass rose below.

Step 1 Find the letter N. That stands for the direction **north**.

Step 2 Find the letters NW. They stand for the direction **northwest**. It is between north and west.

Step 3 Point to the letters SW for **southwest**. Point to the letters SE and NE. Say the directions they stand for.

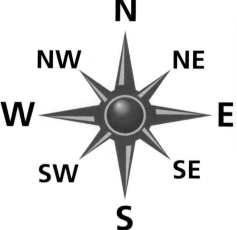

Practice the Skill

Look at the map. Use the compass rose on the map.

1 Put your finger on Savannah. Move your finger along to Macon. In what direction did you move?

2 Move your finger from Augusta to Columbus. In what direction did you move?

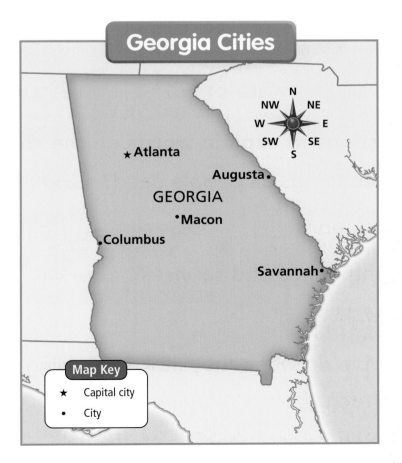

Georgia Cities

★ Atlanta

Augusta •

GEORGIA

• Macon

• Columbus

Savannah •

Map Key
★ Capital city
• City

Big Idea

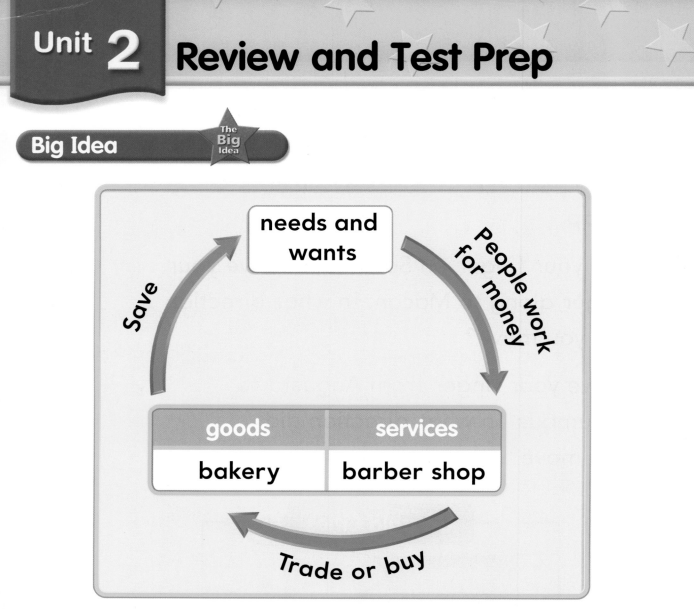

Answer the questions to explain words on the chart.

1. What are three things all people need? (page 70)

2. People work to earn _____. (page 78)

3. What are some goods and services? (page 79)

Facts and Main Ideas

4. What do people do when they make spending choices? (page 72)

5. What are the costs and benefits of saving? (page 87)

Vocabulary

Write the letter or word for each answer.

6. Someone who makes goods or gives services

7. A place where people make goods

8. To put away and keep

9. Someone who buys or uses goods and services

> **A. factory** (page 92)
> **B. producer** (page 90)
> **C. consumer** (page 90)
> **D. benefit** (page 86)
> **E. save** (page 87)

✓ **Test Practice**

10. What does the word **scarcity** mean?

    A. Having a lot of goods
    B. Things people buy and sell
    C. Not having enough of something
    D. A kind of service job people have

Critical Thinking

Compare and Contrast

11. What is the same and different about saving and spending?

12. What was the same about the work George Washington Carver did with sweet potatoes and peanuts?

Review and Test Prep

Use a Compass Rose

This map shows Jenny's neighborhood.

13. What direction does Jenny walk from her house to the library?

14. What is south of the library?

15. What is north of the library?

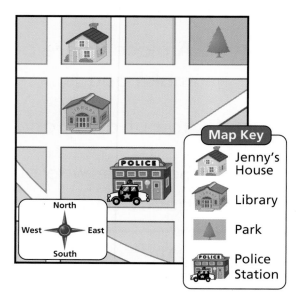

Use Intermediate Directions

16. Name the four intermediate directions.

17. What is the intermediate direction between north and east?

18. What do the letters SW mean?

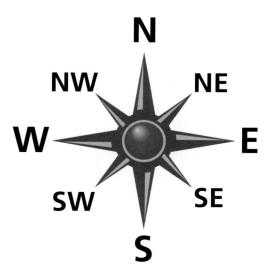

Connect to Georgia

Unit Activity

Georgia Goods

Find out some goods that come from factories or farms in Georgia. Draw pictures of the goods.

1. Tell if they come from a factory or a farm.

2. Add the pictures to a mural that shows goods produced in Georgia.

CURRENT EVENTS
WEEKLY (WR) READER

Current Events Project

Find out about jobs near where you live. Make a **Service Jobs** chart.

Services
dentist
barber
mail carrier

Technology

Read articles about current events at www.eduplace.com/kids/hmss/

Personal Finance

$ GEORGIA

If you earned $5, what would you do with it? How much would you save and how much would you spend?

American Heroes
Read About It

Learn more about George Washington Carver in his biography.

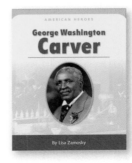

AMERICAN HEROES
George Washington
Carver
By Lisa Zamosky

UNIT 3

Heroes Change America

"Where liberty is, there is my country."
—Benjamin Franklin

The
Big
Idea

In what ways do people and things change over time?

Vocabulary Preview

Technology
e • **glossary**
e • **word games**
www.eduplace.com/kids/hmss/

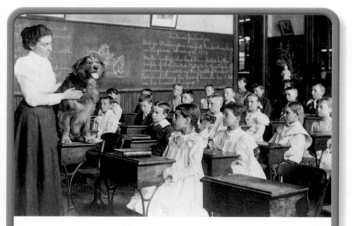

history

History is the story of people and things from the past. page 115

settler

A **settler** is someone who comes to live in a new place. page 123

Reading Strategy

Monitor and Clarify Use the monitor and clarify strategy in Lessons 1 and 2.
Summarize Use the summarize strategy in Lessons 3 and 4.

transportation

Transportation is a way to move people and things from place to place. A train is one kind of transportation. page 134

communication

Communication is a way people share news and ideas. A phone call is one kind of communication. page 142

Learning About the Past

Vocabulary

present

past

history

future

Reading Skill
Compare and Contrast

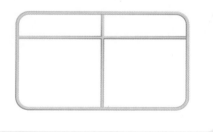

Build on What You Know

Think of something fun you did last summer. That fun time happened before today.

Past and Present

The **present** is what is happening today. The **past** is what happened before today. What is something you can do now that you could not do in the past?

main idea

In the past you were smaller. In the present you are getting taller.

STANDARDS

Core
SS1H1 American history

Extend
SS1H1 American history

A Story of the Past

History tells a story of the past. Your family has a history. Here are three ways to find out about the past.

Talk to people about the past.

Read books or listen to stories about the past.

Look at real things and pictures from the past.

Review What can you do to find out about your family history?

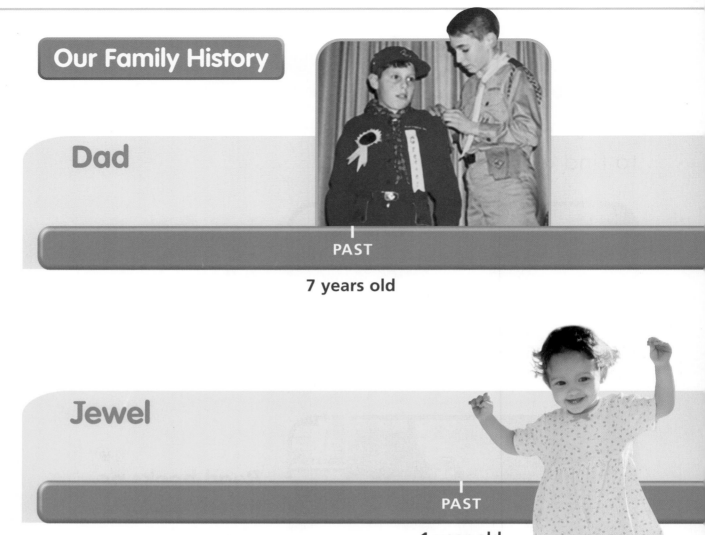

Our Family History

Dad

PAST

7 years old

Jewel

PAST

1 year old

Future

The **future** is the time after today. Tomorrow, next week, and next year are all in the future. In the future you will get bigger and go on to other schools.

main idea (★)

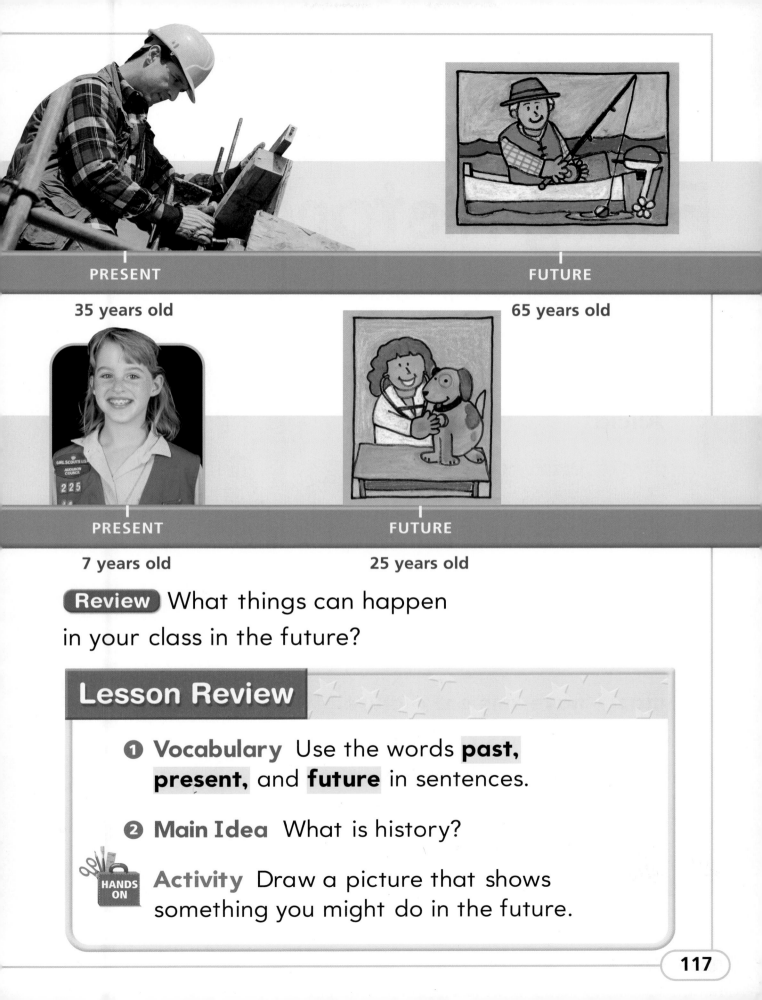

PRESENT

FUTURE

35 years old

65 years old

PRESENT

FUTURE

7 years old

25 years old

Review What things can happen in your class in the future?

Lesson Review

❶ **Vocabulary** Use the words **past, present,** and **future** in sentences.

❷ **Main Idea** What is history?

HANDS ON **Activity** Draw a picture that shows something you might do in the future.

Readers' Theater

Family History Day

Cast

Narrator	**Sam**
Alicia	**Liz**

Narrator: Today is Family History Day at school. Some of us brought things from our families.

Alicia: I have this old picture. It is my grandpa's first car. That's my grandpa when he was young.

Sam: I have this old bank. My mom had it when she was seven. You put money in the elephant's trunk. Then the elephant throws it into the bank.

Liz: This is an old puppet my grandma had.

Narrator: What could you bring to Family History Day?

Activities

1. **Draw It** Draw a picture of something you could bring to Family History Day.

2. **Act It Out** Act the part of someone in your family's history.

Read a Timeline

▶ **Vocabulary**
timeline

A **timeline** shows when things happened. It shows what happened first, next, and last.

Learn the Skill

Step 1 This timeline shows Marco's week at school. The week started on Monday. It ended on Friday.

Step 2 Read what Marco did on each day of the week. Start at the beginning of the week, Monday.

Step 3 Tell what Marco did on Monday, Tuesday, and Wednesday. Use the words **first**, **next**, and **last** to tell when things happened.

Monday

I planted seeds.

Practice the Skill

Look at the timeline again. Then follow the directions.

1 Tell what Marco did on Thursday and Friday. Use the words **first** and **last** to tell the order that things happened.

2 Tell about each thing that happened on Wednesday, Thursday, and Friday. Use the words **first**, **next**, and **last**.

Marco's Week at School

Tuesday	Wednesday	Thursday	Friday
I fed the pet.	I read a book.	I wrote a letter.	I played on the swings.

121

Core Lesson 2

Living in the Past

Vocabulary

settler

explorer

Reading Skill

Compare and Contrast

STANDARDS

Core
SS1H1b Compare everyday life
SS1G1 Cultural and geographic systems

Extend
SS1H1a William Clark, Meriwether Lewis, Sacagawea
SS1G1 Geographic systems

Build on What You Know

Think about moving to a new place. When you move, what are some things that can change?

Pilgrims sailed on a ship called the Mayflower.

New Families Arrive

American Indians were the first people living in North America. Then people from Europe came to trade and fish. Soon families from Europe came here to live. (⭐ main idea)

The Pilgrims were settlers who came from the country of England. A **settler** is a person who comes to live in a new place. The Pilgrims came to be free to practice their beliefs in God. The Pilgrims met the Wampanoag who were living on the land.

Review Where did the Pilgrims come from?

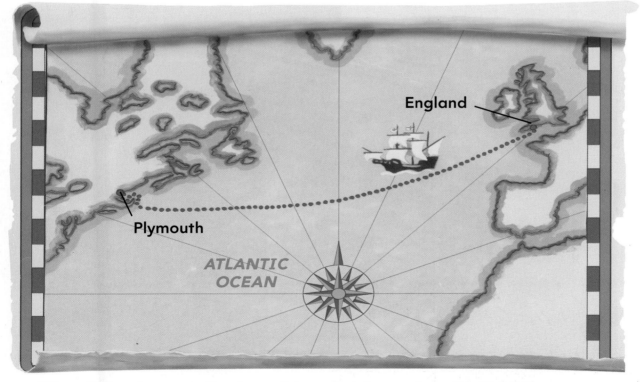

The Pilgrims sailed to North America in 1620.

	Family Life Today
food	
shelter	
clothing	

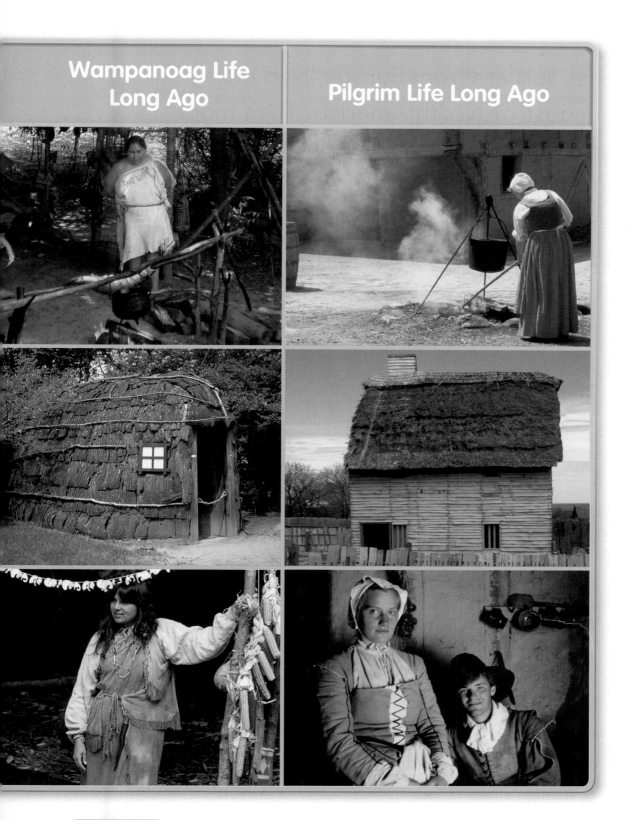

| Wampanoag Life Long Ago | Pilgrim Life Long Ago |

Review In what ways is family life today the same or different from the past?

Moving West

The first settlers from Europe lived along the east coast of North America. Then more and more settlers came to North America. Some settlers and explorers began to travel west. An **explorer** is someone who looks for new places or new things. The land and water were different from in the east.

main idea ★

Many settlers crossed mountains and plains in wagons pulled by strong animals.

Exploring the West

Some settlers who moved west came to a big river called the Mississippi. A few explorers traveled west of the Mississippi. They followed rivers and climbed high mountains. Finally they reached the Pacific Ocean. They made maps that helped others travel west.

main idea

Review What did some explorers do that helped others?

Settlers built towns in the west.

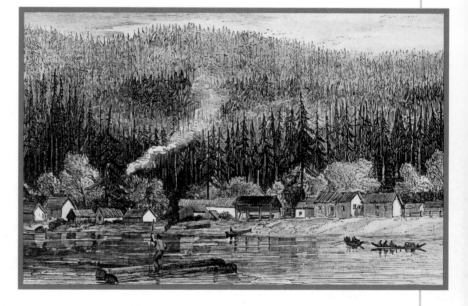

Lesson Review

❶ **Vocabulary** Tell what a **settler** is.

❷ **Main Idea** What did some explorers do in North America?

Activity Draw a picture of something people did in the past. Compare it with something people do today.

Brave Leaders

After more than a year of hard travel, a group of explorers reached the Pacific Ocean. Who helped lead them?

Lewis and Clark

Explorers Lewis and Clark planned and led the trip. On the trip, William Clark made maps of the rivers, lakes, mountains, and plains. Both explorers showed perseverance. They traveled thousands of miles and never gave up.

Meriwether Lewis

William Clark

★ Our Country's Heroes ★

Explorers reach coast ③

Columbia R.

Yellowstone River

ROCKY MOUNTAINS

PACIFIC OCEAN

② Sacagawea joins explorers

Missouri River

GREAT PLAINS

Explorers begin ①

Mississippi River

ATLANTIC OCEAN

Map Key
— Explorers' route
∼ River
⌃⌃ Mountain

N
NW NE
W   E
SW SE
S

The map shows the route the explorers took to the Pacific Ocean.

Both explorers kept journals. This is a page from Clark's journal.

Sacagawea

Sacagawea (sak uh guh WEE uh) joined Lewis and Clark on their trip. She helped the explorers and American Indian groups understand each other. Sacagawea found plants for food and medicine. Her courage helped at many times. Both explorers wrote about important things she did.

> "... [Sacagawea told] me that there was a large road passing through the upper part of this low plain ..."
> —William Clark, July 14, 1806

Sacagawea is honored on a U.S. coin.

Lewis

Clark

Sacagawea

Biographies!
Read more about
Lewis, Clark, and
Sacagawea.

Lewis and Clark
with Sacagawea

By Vicky Willows

Activities

1. Think About It In what ways
were Lewis, Clark, and
Sacagawea alike?

2. Act It Out Walk like you are
exploring a new place that
Lewis and Clark saw. Describe
something you might see.

Use Primary and Secondary Sources

▶ **Vocabulary**

primary source

secondary source

Lewis and Clark wrote about their travels. These writings are primary sources. A **primary source** is writing or telling about an event by someone who was there. A **secondary source** is writing or telling about an event by someone who was not there.

1

"… before me at Some distance (Sacagawea) danced for the joyful sight, and She made signs to me that they were her nation…"

—from William Clark's journal, August 17, 1805

2

Sacagawea had not seen her brother for five years. Then, in August 1805, she happily came to the Shoshone village where he was the leader.

—from a biography of Sacagawea written in 2005

Learn the Skill

Step 1 Read the two sources. What are they about?

Step 2 Point to the words that tell when each source was written.

Step 3 Look for the word *me* in the first source. The word *me* helps you know that William Clark was there.

Practice the Skill

Answer these questions about the two sources.

1 Which one is the primary source? How can you tell?

2 Which one is the secondary source? How can you tell?

3 What is the same about the two sources?

Moving People and Things

Vocabulary
transportation
invention

Reading Skill
Sequence

STANDARDS

Core
SS1H1b Transportation, historical and present

Extend
SS1H1b Everyday life in the present

Build on What You Know

Did you ride the bus to school today? A bus is one way to move from home to school.

Transportation

Long ago, people walked or rode on animals to get around. Transportation was very slow then. **Transportation** is the way we move people and things.

main idea (★)

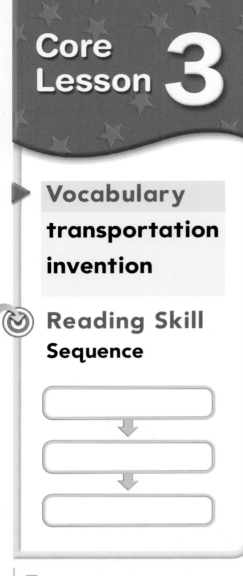

Inventions

People made inventions because they wanted better transportation. An **invention** is a new tool or way of doing something. Trains, cars, and airplanes were all inventions at one time. Some inventions make moving people and things faster and easier.

(⭐) main idea

Orville and Wilbur Wright invented an airplane.

Review Why do you think people make inventions?

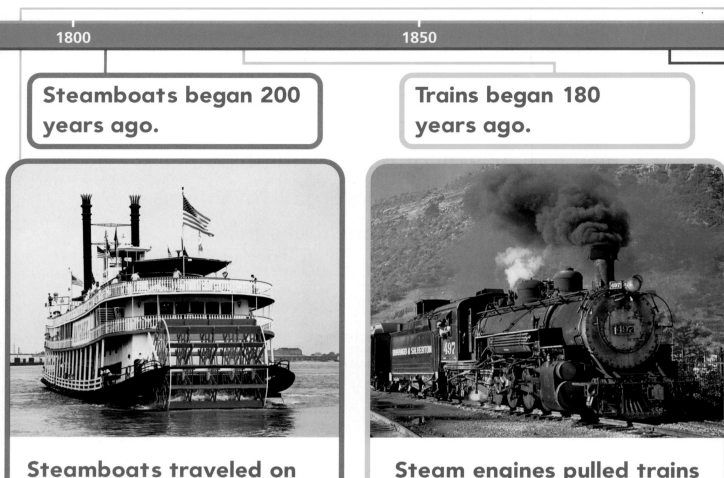

1800 **1850**

Steamboats began 200 years ago.

Trains began 180 years ago.

Steamboats traveled on rivers from city to city.

Steam engines pulled trains on railroads.

Transportation Changes

Transportation keeps changing. Trains, planes, and high speed boats help people travel anywhere on Earth. It takes less time to move people and things than ever before.

main ★ idea

Review How do transportation inventions change the way people live?

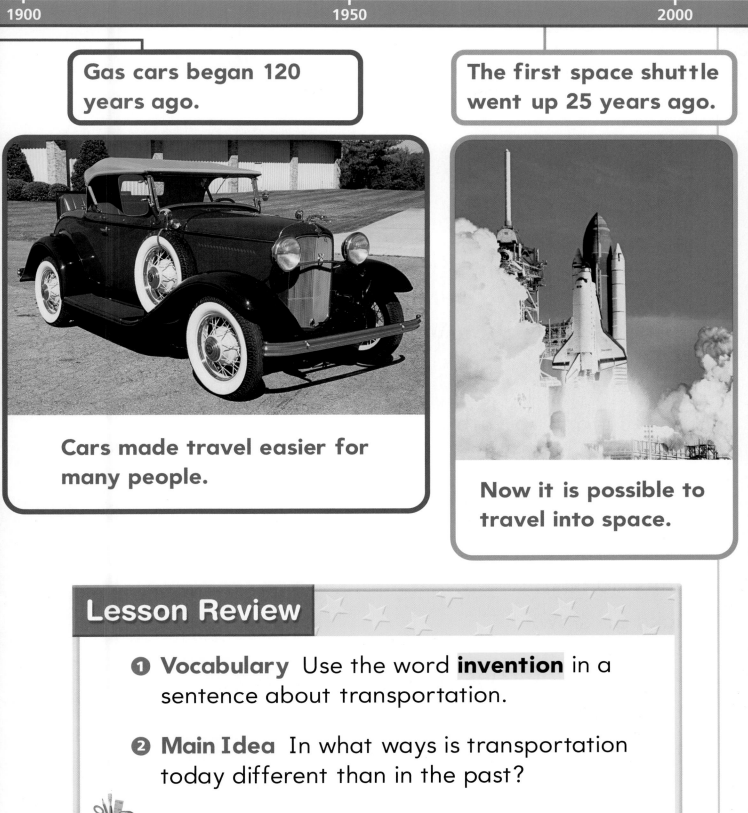

1900   1950   2000

Gas cars began 120 years ago.

Cars made travel easier for many people.

The first space shuttle went up 25 years ago.

Now it is possible to travel into space.

Lesson Review

❶ **Vocabulary** Use the word **invention** in a sentence about transportation.

❷ **Main Idea** In what ways is transportation today different than in the past?

HANDS ON

Activity Draw the kinds of transportation you use.

Literature

Rush Hour

by Christine Loomis

Do you hurry to get to school? That is a busy rush hour for you.

Engines start up with a jerk.
People hurry off to work.

Horns go beep-beep,
whistles blow,
Planes go fast,
Trucks go slow.

Trolleys sway, ferries rock,
Time keeps ticking
On the clock.

Cars on side streets,
Trains on tracks,
Whizzing,
Zipping,
Clicky
Clack,
Rumbling,
Roaring,
Jiggling,
Jumping,
Left turn,
Right turn,
Backing,
Bumping.

Activities

1. **Talk About It** Describe things and people in the picture that go with words in the poem.

2. **Write It** Write a short poem about one kind of transportation in the picture.

Tell Fact from Opinion

▶ **Vocabulary**

fact
opinion

A **fact** is something that is true. An **opinion** is what someone thinks. People may have different opinions.

Learn the Skill

Step 1 Read the two sentences. One gives a fact. One gives an opinion.

Step 2 Opinions use words such as "I think." Point to the sentence with the words "I think."

Step 3 You can check if a fact is true. Point to the sentence that gives a fact that you can check.

A I think trains are more fun than cars.

B Trains were an invention that came before cars.

Practice the Skill

Answer these questions about the two sentences.

1 Which one gives a fact? Check the fact by looking at the timeline on pages 136 and 137.

2 Which one gives an opinion? How can you tell?

3 What is the same about the two sentences?

Sharing News and Ideas

Vocabulary
communicate
communication

Reading Skill
Sequence

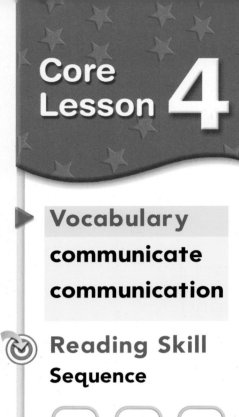

⬛ **STANDARDS**

Core
SS1H1b Communication: compare past and present

Extend
SS1H1a Benjamin Franklin, inventor, author,
   statesman
SS1H1b Everyday life: compare past and present
SS1CG1 Character trait: commitment

Build on What You Know

Do you talk on the telephone? Using the telephone is one way to share news.

People Share News

When people tell what they know, they **communicate.** Two ways to communicate are talking and writing. The way people *main idea* ⭐ share news and ideas is called **communication.**

Long ago, town criers called out the news.

People's Lives Change

Books are a way to share ideas. Long ago, people wrote books by hand. Writing the pages of just one book would take many weeks. To make a copy took more weeks.

An invention called the printing press changed people's lives. With a printing press, workers made copies of the same book much more quickly. Then more people had books to read and learn from. More people could communicate what they learned.

Review In what ways do you communicate?

This large machine is a printing press from the past.

Inventions Timeline

| 100 years ago | 80 years ago | 60 years ago |

Alexander Graham Bell invented the telephone more than 100 years ago. People could talk to friends near and far using the telephone.

The first television let people see and hear news and shows in their homes.

The radio brought news and shows to people's homes.

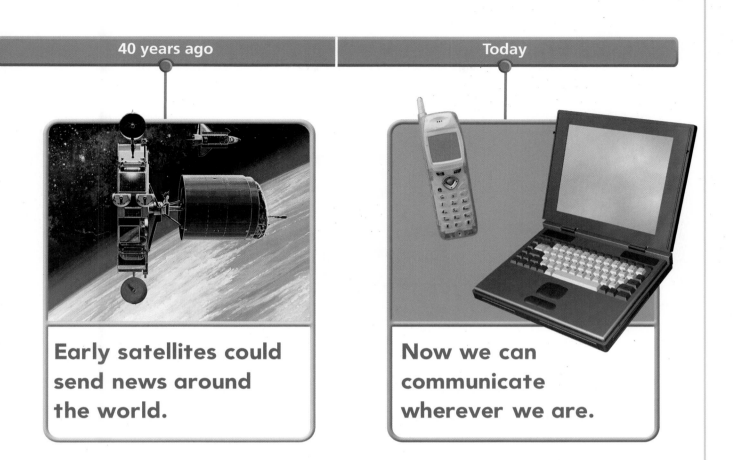

| 40 years ago | Today |

Early satellites could send news around the world.

Now we can communicate wherever we are.

Review Tell ways that communication has changed from the past.

Lesson Review

❶ **Vocabulary** Name the ways you **communicate** with your friends.

❷ **Main Idea** What are two inventions that helped people communicate?

HANDS ON

Activity Make a chart of inventions that you use for communication.

Benjamin Franklin

Benjamin Franklin had three amazing skills. He was an author and wrote books that people loved. He was also an inventor. He invented special eyeglasses called bifocals. Franklin was a leader, too. He helped start the United States of America.

Benjamin Franklin showed commitment by always working to help others.

Franklin once wrote,

" . . . write things worth reading or do things worth the writing."

★ Our Country's Heroes ★

Benjamin
Franklin

Franklin was one of our
country's first leaders.

Biographies!
Read more about
Benjamin Franklin.

AMERICAN HEROES
Benjamin
Franklin

By Lynne Green

Activities

1. **Talk About It** What were
   Franklin's three amazing skills?

2. **Write About It** Why do you
   think Benjamin Franklin was
   a hero?

Big Idea

The Big Idea

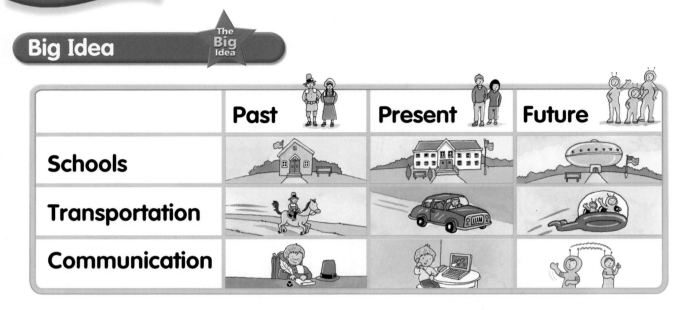

	Past	Present	Future
Schools			
Transportation			
Communication			

Fill in the missing words that help describe the chart.

1. The _____ is time that has not happened yet. (page 116)
2. In the past, people used horses for _____. (page 134)
3. In the present, we use computers and telephones for _____. (page 145)

Facts and Main Ideas

4. How do we learn about the past? (page 115)

5. What are two things that are different about your life and the lives of people in the past? (pages 124 to 125)

6. What kinds of transportation today are faster than transportation long ago? (pages 135 to 137)

7. What are some communication inventions you use every day? (pages 144 and 145)

Vocabulary

Write the letter for each correct answer.

8. A new way of doing something

9. The time that is now

10. A story about the past

11. Sharing news and ideas

A. history (page 115)

B. present (page 114)

C. invention (page 135)

D. communication (page 142)

E. transportation (page 134)

✔ Test Practice

12. What does the word **explorer** mean?

    A. Someone who comes to live in a new place

    B. Someone who looks for new places or new things

    C. A way to share news and ideas

    D. A place where settlers live

Critical Thinking   Sequence

13. What did Lewis and Clark do before Sacagawea began to travel with them?

14. What did Benjamin Franklin do before America became a country?

Skillbuilders

Read a Timeline

The Pilgrims' Farming Timeline

1621

Spring   Summer   Fall

15. What did the Pilgrims do first?

16. What happened during the summer?

Identify Fact and Opinion

A. Orville and Wilbur Wright invented an airplane.

B. I think airplanes were the best invention.

17. Which sentence above gives an opinion? Which words tell you it is an opinion?

18. Which sentence gives a fact? Check the fact on page 135.

Connect to Georgia

Unit Activity

Make an Accordion Book

Think about changes in your community or another place in Georgia.

1 Fold a sheet of paper in four parts.

2 Draw and write about your community's past, present, and future.

Personal Finance

What choices about spending money in a family today might be different from choices in a Pilgrim family?

WEEKLY (WR) READER

Current Events

Find out about people from the past who may be in the news today. Make **History Puppets.**

Technology

Read articles about current events at www.eduplace.com/kids/hmss/

American Heroes
Read About It

Learn more about Lewis and Clark with Sacagawea, and Benjamin Franklin in their biographies.

UNIT 4

Good Citizens

"The government is us.
We are the government,
you and I."

—Theodore Roosevelt

The Big Idea

What do good
citizens do?

Vocabulary Preview

Technology
e • **glossary**
e • **word games**
www.eduplace.com/kids/hmss/

government

The leader of a **government** helps to run a community, a state, or a country.

page 157

President

The **President** is the leader of the United States government. Thomas Jefferson was the third President.

page 165

Reading Strategy

Question Use the question strategy in Lessons 1 and 2.
Predict and Infer Use the predict and infer strategy in Lessons 3 and 4.

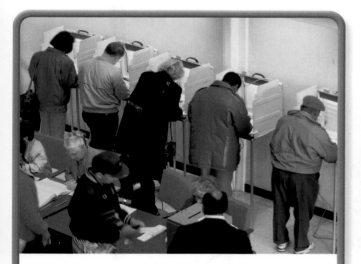

vote

When people **vote,** they make a choice.

page 170

symbol

The flag is a **symbol** of our country. It stands for freedom.

page 174

People Need Laws

Vocabulary
law
government

Reading Skill
Draw Conclusions

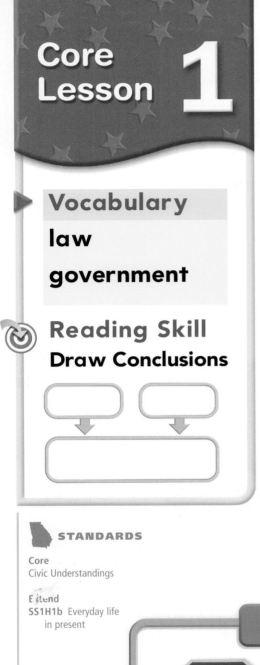

STANDARDS

Core
Civic Understandings

Extend
SS1H1b Everyday life
in present

Build on What You Know

What class rules do you follow? Did you know that communities have written rules too?

Laws

A community rule is called a **law.** A community needs laws. Laws help keep a community safe, clean, and fair for everyone.

main idea

Signs That Show Laws

STOP

All cars must stop.

Children cross here.

NO PARKING ANY TIME

Do not park here.

People Help With Laws

A **government** is a group of people chosen to make laws. There are community, state, and country governments. People can work to make and to change laws.

The crossing guard is a community helper.

Review What are ways people help with laws?

Lesson Review

❶ **Vocabulary** Tell about one **law** in your community.

❷ **Main Idea** Why does a community need laws?

HANDS ON **Activity** Make a sign that shows a law in your community.

Laws Every Day

Breakfast Time

Food Laws

Many foods must have labels. A label shows what was used to make the food.

Nutrition Facts

Serving Size   1 cup

Servings Per Container   About 17

Ingredients

Corn Flour

Wheat Flour

Brown Sugar

School Time

Bus Laws

The stop sign on a bus tells cars to stop so children can be safe.

STOP

Play Time

Toy Laws

Labels tell how to use toys safely. They tell how old a child should be to use the toy.

WARNING

not for children under age 3

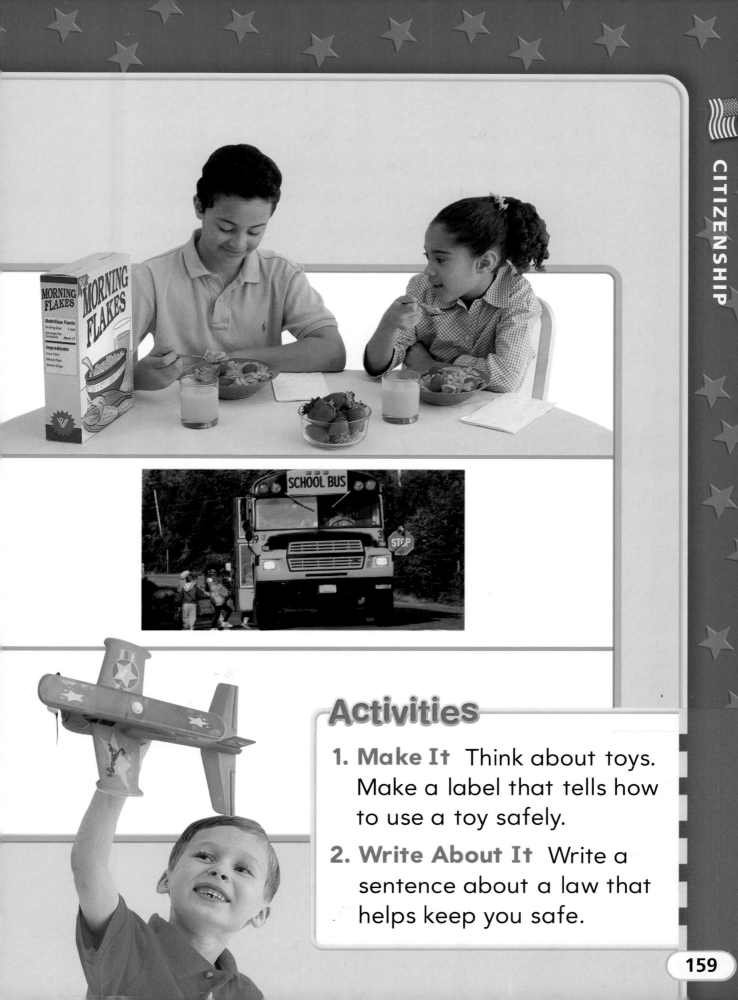

Activities

1. **Make It** Think about toys. Make a label that tells how to use a toy safely.

2. **Write About It** Write a sentence about a law that helps keep you safe.

Solve a Problem

▶ Vocabulary
problem

When people do not agree, they have a **problem.** Families can find ways to solve problems.

Learn the Skill

Follow the steps to solve a problem.

Step 1 One child wants to go to the toy store. The other wants to go to the pet store. Tell what the problem is.

Step 2 Think of some ways the family could help to solve the problem.

- Go to the toy store today and the pet store tomorrow.

- Go to both stores today.

Step 3 Which way would you choose?

Practice the Skill

Look at the picture below. Read the words.

Then follow the directions.

1 Tell what the problem is.

2 Think of some ways to try to solve
the problem.

3 Choose one way to solve the problem.
Tell why it is a good way.

It's time to
eat dinner.

I'd like to eat
dinner next door
at Evan's house.

Government and Leaders

▶ **Vocabulary**

mayor

governor

President

⊙ **Reading Skill**
**Main idea and
Details**

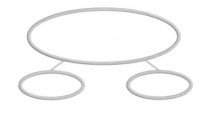

Build on What You Know

Your teacher is a leader. Governments have leaders too.

Government

There are governments of cities and towns, of states, and of the country. Each place has a main government building.

Your community may have a city or town hall. There is a capitol building in your state.

The White House and other government buildings for the country are in Washington, D.C.

STANDARDS

Core
SS1CG1 Positive character traits

Extend
SS1H1a Thomas Jefferson (Declaration of Independence)
SS1H1b Historical figures
SS1CG1 Character trait: fairness

City or town hall

State capitol building

White House

Review What are names of buildings where government leaders work?

Government Leaders

In the United States, government leaders are chosen by the people. Each leader works to make our country a good place to live.

Mayor

A **mayor** is the leader of a city or town government. A community government has many services, such as schools and libraries. Mayors need to be fair to everyone in a community.

City Mayor

Governor

A **governor** is the leader of a state government. State governments have services such as state roads, colleges, and parks. Governors try to show respect for land and water in their states.

State Governor

President

The **President** is the leader of the United States government. The President helps to make laws for all people in the United States. A President must show commitment to the country.

President of the United States

Review What does the President of the United States do?

Lesson Review

1 **Vocabulary** Tell something you know about a **governor.**

2 **Main Idea** What is different about the work of a mayor, a governor, and the President?

Activity Draw and name a government building.

Thomas Jefferson

Thomas Jefferson wrote important words called the Declaration of Independence. Jefferson believed in fairness. He wrote that the people of America wanted liberty, or freedom to rule themselves. They wanted England to stop ruling them. American leaders signed the Declaration and sent it to the king of England.

The Declaration of Independence started the United States of America.

★ Our Country's Heroes ★

Benjamin Franklin

John Adams

Thomas Jefferson

These leaders talked about the words.

Biographies!
Read more about
Thomas Jefferson.

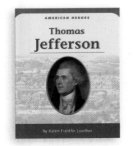

AMERICAN HEROES
Thomas
Jefferson

By Karen Franklin Lowther

Activities

1. **Talk About It** What do you see in the leaders' hands in the picture?

2. **Act It Out** Show and tell what one of the leaders in the picture might say.

Core Lesson 3

Vocabulary

right

responsibility

vote

election

Reading Skill

Main Idea and Details

STANDARDS

Core
SS1H1b Life in the present
SS1CG1 Positive character traits

Extend
SS1H1a Harriet Tubman
SS1H1b Historical figures
SS1CG1 Character trait: equality

Citizens

Build on What You Know

Why is it important to be a good helper in your community and in our country?

Citizens Have Rights

Citizens of the United States have rights. A **right** is something you are free to do.

Betsy and Dan Nally collect turkeys and give them to families who have no money to buy Thanksgiving dinner.

Citizens Have Responsibilities

Citizens have responsibilities. A **responsibility** is a duty to do something. One responsibility citizens have is to help to make laws and to follow them. Good citizens can help make their country a better place to live.

main (★) idea

Review What are some ways that you can be a good citizen?

Citizens Make Choices

Sometimes people in a group want to do different things. People can vote to decide which thing to do. When people **vote,** they make a choice. Voting is a fair way for groups to make decisions.

main idea (★)

Tim votes to go to the aquarium. He will put his ballot in the box.

Ballot
Where will we go for our field Trip?
☒ Aquarium
☐ Dairy farm

Ballot Box

Citizens choose their government leaders in an election. An **election** is a time when citizens vote for the leader they think will do the best job. The winner is the one with the most votes. Citizens can vote for rules and laws too. Voting is a responsibility.

Review What things have you voted on in school?

Lesson Review

1 Vocabulary What do citizens **vote** for in an election?

2 Main Idea What responsibilities does a citizen have?

Activity Write about a field trip you would vote for. Why is that a good choice?

Harriet Tubman

Long ago, Harriet Tubman led hundreds of people to freedom. First she escaped from a life where African Americans were forced to work without pay. Because she believed in equality, she went back to lead others north to freedom. The way they traveled was called the Underground Railroad. Mostly they walked, but they were like passengers on a secret train. Tubman said,

"I never lost a passenger."

★ Our Country's Heroes ★

This statue reminds people that Tubman knew safe routes for children and adults.

Biographies!
Read more about
Harriet Tubman.

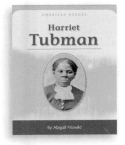

Activities

1. **Act It Out**
   What do you think Harriet Tubman and the boy are saying?

2. **Write About It**
   Write a sentence that tells something you learned about Harriet Tubman.

Core Lesson 4

Symbols of Our Country

Vocabulary
symbol
honor

Reading Skill
Classify

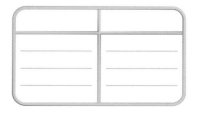

Build on What You Know

Where have you seen the flag of our country?

Stars and Stripes

Our flag is a symbol for our country. A **symbol** is a picture, place, or thing that stands for something else.

The American Flag

STANDARDS

Core
SS1H1 Historical figures
SS1G1 Geographic systems

Extend
SS1H1 Historical figures

The flag has red and white stripes. It has 50 stars, one for each state.

Uncle Sam is also a symbol. The first letters of Uncle Sam are the same as in the words United States.

Review Why do you think Uncle Sam is dressed as he is?

This boy is dressed as Uncle Sam.

Symbols of Freedom

We **honor** symbols of the United States to show that our country is important to us. The Liberty Bell and the bald eagle are symbols of freedom.

The Liberty Bell

The bald eagle stands for a strong country.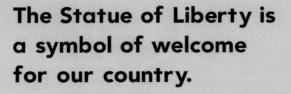

The Statue of Liberty is a symbol of welcome for our country.

Review What symbols have you seen?

Places As Symbols

Places and buildings can be symbols too. For example, the Lincoln Memorial honors President Abraham Lincoln. The Washington Monument honors President George Washington. Look at the map of Washington, D.C. Find these buildings on the map.

The White House is in Washington, D.C.

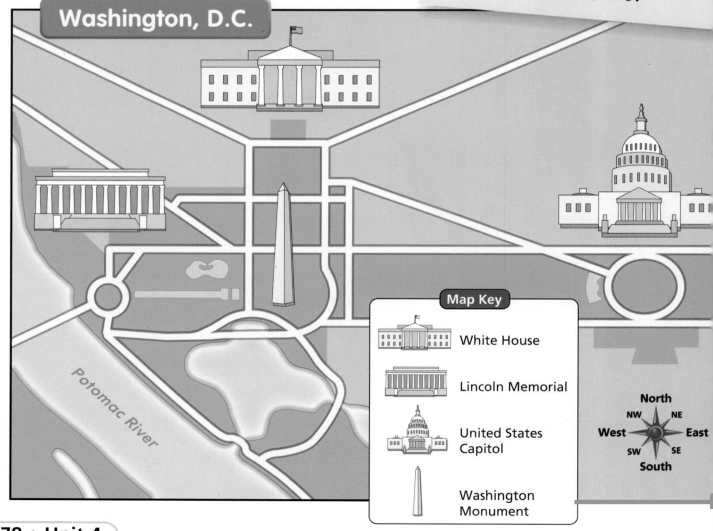

Washington, D.C.

Potomac River

Map Key

White House

Lincoln Memorial

United States Capitol

Washington Monument

North
NW   NE
West ——— East
SW   SE
South

The Lincoln Memorial is also in Washington, D.C.

Mount Rushmore shows the faces of four past Presidents.

Review Name a place that is a symbol for our country.

Lesson Review

❶ **Vocabulary** Tell why we **honor** symbols of our country.

❷ **Main Idea** Why does our country have symbols?

Activity Write about three symbols you like.

George Washington

George Washington was the first President of the United States. He is known as the Father of His Country because he was the first leader of our new country.

President George Washington made a promise to follow the Constitution. The Constitution is a plan for making laws for the United States. Every new President makes the same promise.

The Constitution of the United States of America.

Activities

1. **Talk About It** Tell something you see in the picture of George Washington.

2. **Make It** Make a fact card about George Washington.

Big Idea

Responsible Citizens

A.   B.

Match the words to the correct picture above.

1. follow laws (page 156)

2. vote (page 170)

Facts and Main Ideas

3. Why do communities need laws? (page 156)

4. What is the same about community, state, and country governments? (page 157)

5. Name one right and two responsibilities that citizens have in the United States. (pages 168–169)

6. What is an election? (page 171)

Vocabulary

Write the letter or word for each correct answer.

7. A community rule is called a _____ .

8. The flag is a _____ of our country.

9. The leader of a state is called the _____ .

A. **governor** (page 164)

B. **law** (page 156)

C. **symbol** (page 174)

D. **President** (page 175)

E. **government** (page 157)

✓ Test Practice

10. The word **election** means _____ .

A. the leader of a state

B. someone who is a hero

C. a time when people vote

D. a symbol of our country

Critical Thinking

Summarize

11. What did Thomas Jefferson do that helped America?

12. What did Harriet Tubman do for many people?

Solve a Problem

Lisa says, "I want to buy a real dog. My brother wants to buy a toy horse. My dad says we only have enough money to buy one of those."

13. Tell what problem Lisa's family has.

14. What are two ways to solve the problem?

15. Choose one of the two ways. Tell why you think it is a good way.

Connect to Georgia

Unit Activity

Make a Leaders Chart

Think of leaders in your community, in Georgia, and in the United States.

❶ Write the words **Our Leaders** on the top of a paper.

❷ Make three parts in your chart. Write about a leader in each part.

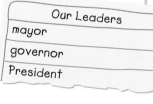

Our Leaders
mayor
governor
President

Personal Finance

In what ways is voting like making a choice about spending money? In what ways is it different? Which one affects more people?

Current Events Project

Find out about heroes in your community. Make biography cards for **Heroes in the News.**

Technology

Read articles about current events at www.eduplace.com/kids/hmss/

American Heroes
Read About It

Learn more about Thomas Jefferson and Harriet Tubman.

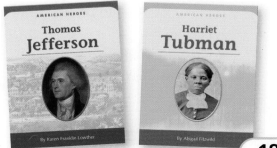

American Folktales

As retold by Leslie Cohen

Folktales are stories people have told and retold over many years. They often have both true and made up parts. Many American folktales are about characters who did amazing things. In these folktales, you will learn more about our country.

John Henry and the Machine

John Henry was a mighty man. He worked on railroads. The railroad boss said, "Take a hammer and spike. Make holes in all these mountain rocks to start a tunnel for the trains."

"I have two hands," said John Henry, "Give me two hammers!" He raised them high. *Whap! Whap!* John Henry hammered all day long.

One day a stranger came. "My machine can do more work than 20 men."

"Let's race," smiled John Henry.

John Henry hammered his spikes deeper and faster than the machine. He was so strong!

"*Hurrah! Hurrah!*" Everyone cheered. Mighty John Henry was mighty happy. Now people still tell how John Henry beat the machine!

Talk About It

1. **What did John Henry do?**

2. **What are some ways people can show they are strong?**

Johnny Appleseed

Johnny got down on his knees. He dug a hole in the dirt. Gently, he placed one apple seed into the hole. He covered and watered the seed. An apple tree would grow from that seed. The tree would give people apples. From the apples they would have new seeds for more trees.

His real name was John Chapman, but people called him Johnny Appleseed. He planted seeds wherever he went. He traveled at a time when settlers were just moving west. He slept under the stars. He sold or gave people the small trees he planted.

Johnny told stories to the children, who loved him. People wanted this caring man to live with them, but Johnny wanted to keep moving. In his mind, he saw all the trees he hoped to plant in other places.

When Johnny Appleseed was done planting, he stood up and smiled. Then as always, he moved on.

Talk About It

1. **What did Johnny Appleseed do?**
2. **Why is it important to be caring?**

Davy Crockett and Raccoon

Davy Crockett was the best hunter in Tennessee. All the animals in the woods knew that. If Davy shot, he never missed.

Furry Raccoon was high up in a tree one day. Raccoon saw Davy, and Davy saw her. Raccoon thought fast. Just as Davy raised his gun, she raised her paw. "Please, Sir, are you Davy Crockett, the best hunter in Tennessee?"

"Yes, I am," said Davy proudly.

"Please, Sir, would you be so kind? I always hoped to shake your hand."

"Sure. Come on down," Davy said.

Raccoon came down from the tree. She looked up at Davy and said, "Oh, Sir, you look so extra tall and strong from here!"

"That's nice to hear," Davy said. He put down his gun to shake her paw.

"You are very kind, Sir," said Raccoon. Slowly she backed away.

"You are kind yourself," said Davy.

"I know that you are very smart, Sir," said Raccoon. All at once she dashed away.

Davy laughed. "You are very smart yourself!" he called out after her.

"Thank you, Sir!" Raccoon called from very far away.

Talk About It

1. **Who was Davy Crockett?**
2. **When does a good joke help people?**

Paul Bunyan and Babe

This tale is as tall as the tallest tree in America. One night on a freezing hot day, a baby boy named Paul Bunyan was born. He was already too big for a crib or a bed. Soon Paul grew too big to fit inside a house or school. He had to stay outside. Paul cut down trees with a BIG ax. He piled up logs higher than the highest mountain. Paul became the BIGGEST and best logger ever, anywhere.

But Paul was lonely. One blue-cold winter, Paul found Babe the Blue Ox. Babe was even bigger than Paul. It took a bird all winter to fly from one of her horns to the other!

Together, Paul and Babe did BIG work. Paul lifted roads. Then Babe pulled hard and made them straight. Babe helped Paul make the Grand Canyon and the Rocky Mountains. Paul and Babe were the BIGGEST friends ever, anywhere.

Talk About It

1. Who was Paul Bunyan?
2. What can friends do by working together?

Annie Oakley and the Contest

Annie stood quietly with her old rifle. Today was her first shooting contest, but she was a great shooter. She had paid for her family's Ohio farm by hunting with her rifle. "I *know* I will win," Annie told herself.

Frank Butler was in the contest, too. He was the best shot around. Frank looked at Annie. "She is small and young. I will certainly win," he thought.

"Pull!" called Frank. A clay target was sent into the air. Frank shot the target into bits.

"Pull!" called Annie. She shot the next target apart. The score was tied, 1 to 1.

The contest went on. Frank shot. Then Annie shot. They hit target after target. Both hit 24 targets and never missed. Finally, Frank missed.

Now it was Annie's turn. Calmly, she said, "Pull!" She shot—and won, 25 to 24!

"That's okay," said Frank. "I have fallen in love with Annie."

One year later, Annie and Frank got married. Together they did shooting tricks in many states and in other countries. Annie Oakley was known as the best shot ever!

Talk About It

1. **Who was Annie Oakley?**
2. **What do people do to become best at a skill?**

American Folktales

★ Activities ★

Now you have read some American folktales. Think of the people and animals in those stories. Here are some ways to share what you liked and learned.

Activity

American Places

1. Choose one of the folktales.

2. Read it again. Find out about the place or places where it happened.

3. Make a big picture of one of the places. Then act out the folktale.

Activity

Learn More

1. At the library find and read more about one of the people in American Folktales.

2. Write a sentence telling about something you learned.

3. Add it to a class book about American folktales.

Activity

Folktale Telling

1. Choose a folktale.

2. In your own words, tell something that happened in the story.

3. In what way is telling the story different from reading the story in a book?

References

Citizenship Handbook

Resources

The Pledge of Allegiance

The pledge is a statement about our country. When we say the Pledge of Allegiance, we show that we care about the United States of America.

The Pledge of Allegiance

I pledge allegiance to the flag
of the United States of America
and to the Republic for which it stands,
one Nation under God, indivisible,
With liberty and justice for all.

Our Flag

How do you feel when you see the American flag flying from a flag pole? Have you ever marched with a flag at school or in a parade? By holding our country's flag high we show we care about the United States.

When we respect the flag, we show pride in the United States. There are rules about how to care for the flag.

The flag must never touch the ground. The flag should be lit at night.

Our Motto

Each country can have its own motto, or saying. A motto reminds people of things that are important to their country. Our country's motto is *e pluribus unum*. This means that Americans can be very different from each other, but we all belong to the same country. The motto is on our coins.

country's motto

Some coins honor people or events. The head of this nickel shows Thomas Jefferson.

R3

Character Traits

A character trait is what you see when a person acts. A person who acts bravely shows courage. Courage is a character trait. Some character traits can help you do your best now and when you get older.

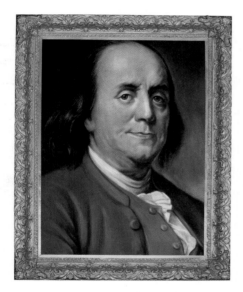

Benjamin Franklin
Commitment means working hard to do something until it is done. Benjamin Franklin worked hard to reach goals for his community and for the United States of America.

Harriet Tubman
Equality means the same treatment for everyone. Harriet Tubman led people from places where they were enslaved to where they could have equal treatment.

Courage means acting bravely. It may take courage to speak up.

Perseverance means doing something even though it is not easy.

Tolerance is respect for beliefs and ideas that are different from yours.

Respect for others means paying attention to what other people want and believe.

Fairness means acting to make things fair, or right, for everyone.

Respect for the environment means caring for nature. Part of this is **conservation**, or using resources carefully.

Geographic Terms

▲ desert
a dry area where plants that need little water grow

forest
a large area of land where many trees grow

hill
a raised mass of land, smaller than a mountain

▲ island
land with water all around it

lake
a body of water with land all around it

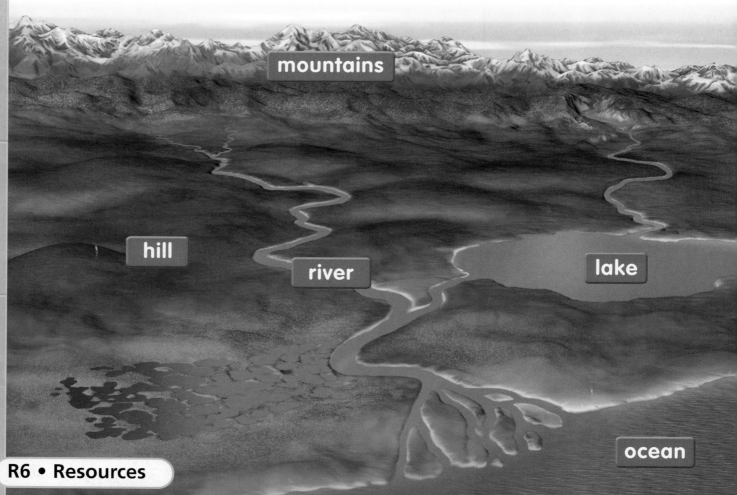

mountains

hill

river

lake

ocean

mountain
a steep mass of land, much higher than the land around it

▲ **ocean**
a salty body of water covering a large area of the earth

peninsula
land that sticks out into water

plain
a broad, flat area of land

plateau
an area of flat land that is higher than the land around it

river
a large stream of water that runs into a lake, ocean, or another river

valley
low land between mountains or hills

valley

plain

peninsula

Atlas The World

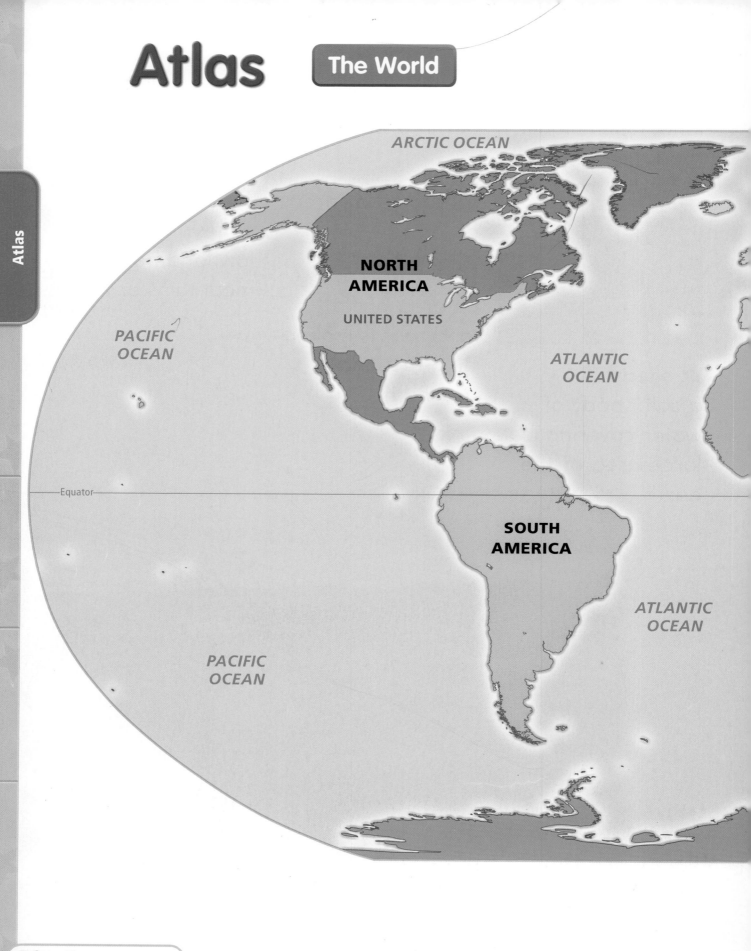

ARCTIC OCEAN

NORTH
AMERICA

UNITED STATES

PACIFIC
OCEAN

ATLANTIC
OCEAN

Equator

SOUTH
AMERICA

ATLANTIC
OCEAN

PACIFIC
OCEAN

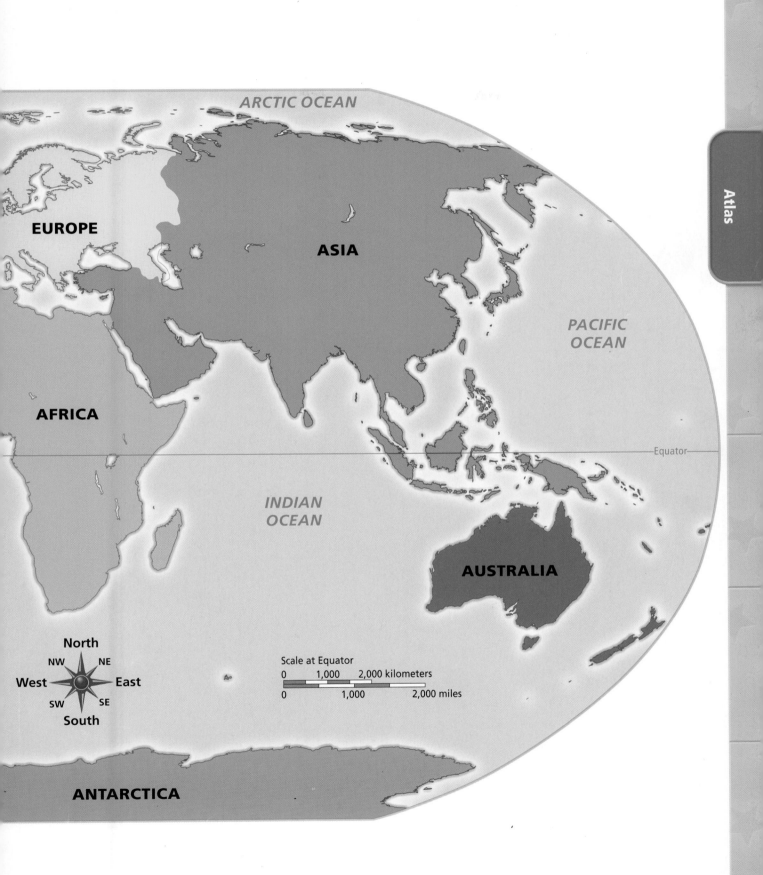

ARCTIC OCEAN

EUROPE

ASIA

PACIFIC
OCEAN

AFRICA

Equator

INDIAN
OCEAN

AUSTRALIA

North
NW   NE
West   East
SW   SE
South

ANTARCTICA

Scale at Equator
0   1,000   2,000 kilometers
0   1,000   2,000 miles

Canada, United States, Mexico

North
NW   NE
West   East
SW   SE
South

PACIFIC OCEAN

Map Key

⊛ National Capital

— National Boundary

0   400   800 kilometers

0   400   800 miles

ARCTIC OCEAN

CANADA

Ottawa
⭐

UNITED STATES

Washington, D.C.
⭐

ATLANTIC
OCEAN

MEXICO

Mexico City
⭐

The United States

ALASKA

0 — 500 kilometers
0 — 500 miles

WASHINGTON

OREGON

IDAHO

MONTANA

WYOMING

NEVADA

UTAH

COLORADO

CALIFORNIA

ARIZONA

NEW MEXICO

North
NW   NE
West   East
SW   SE
South

Map Key
⊛ National Capital
— National Boundary
— State Boundary

HAWAII

0 — 200 kilometers
0 — 200 miles

Atlas

NEW
HAMPSHIRE

VERMONT

MASSACHUSETTS

MAINE

NORTH
DAKOTA

MINNESOTA

SOUTH
DAKOTA

WISCONSIN

MICHIGAN

NEW
YORK

RHODE
ISLAND

CONNECTICUT

NEBRASKA

IOWA

PENNSYLVANIA

NEW
JERSEY

DELAWARE

Washington, D.C.

MARYLAND

ILLINOIS

INDIANA

OHIO

WEST
VIRGINIA

VIRGINIA

KANSAS

MISSOURI

KENTUCKY

NORTH
CAROLINA

TENNESSEE

SOUTH
CAROLINA

OKLAHOMA

ARKANSAS

ALABAMA

GEORGIA

MISSISSIPPI

TEXAS

LOUISIANA

FLORIDA

0   125   250 kilometers
0   125   250 miles

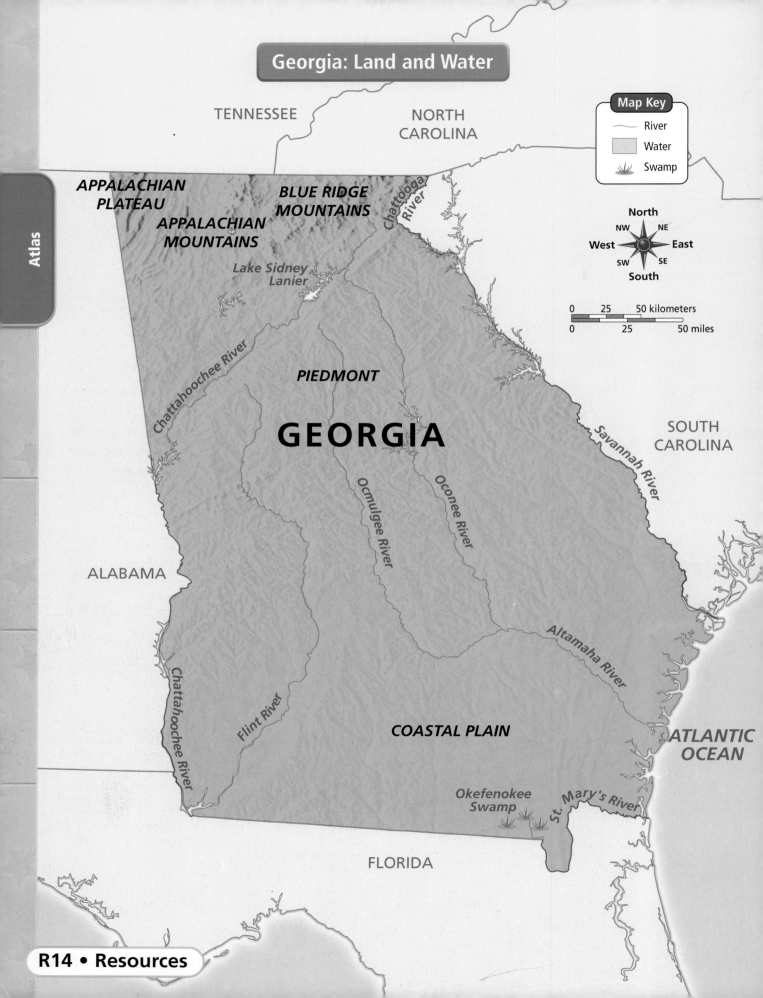

Georgia: Land and Water

TENNESSEE

NORTH CAROLINA

Map Key
- River
- Water
- Swamp

North
NW NE
West East
SW SE
South

0   25   50 kilometers
0   25   50 miles

APPALACHIAN PLATEAU

BLUE RIDGE MOUNTAINS

APPALACHIAN MOUNTAINS

Chattooga River

Lake Sidney Lanier

Chattahoochee River

PIEDMONT

GEORGIA

SOUTH CAROLINA

Savannah River

ALABAMA

Ocmulgee River

Oconee River

Altamaha River

Flint River

Chattahoochee River

COASTAL PLAIN

ATLANTIC OCEAN

Okefenokee Swamp

St. Mary's River

FLORIDA

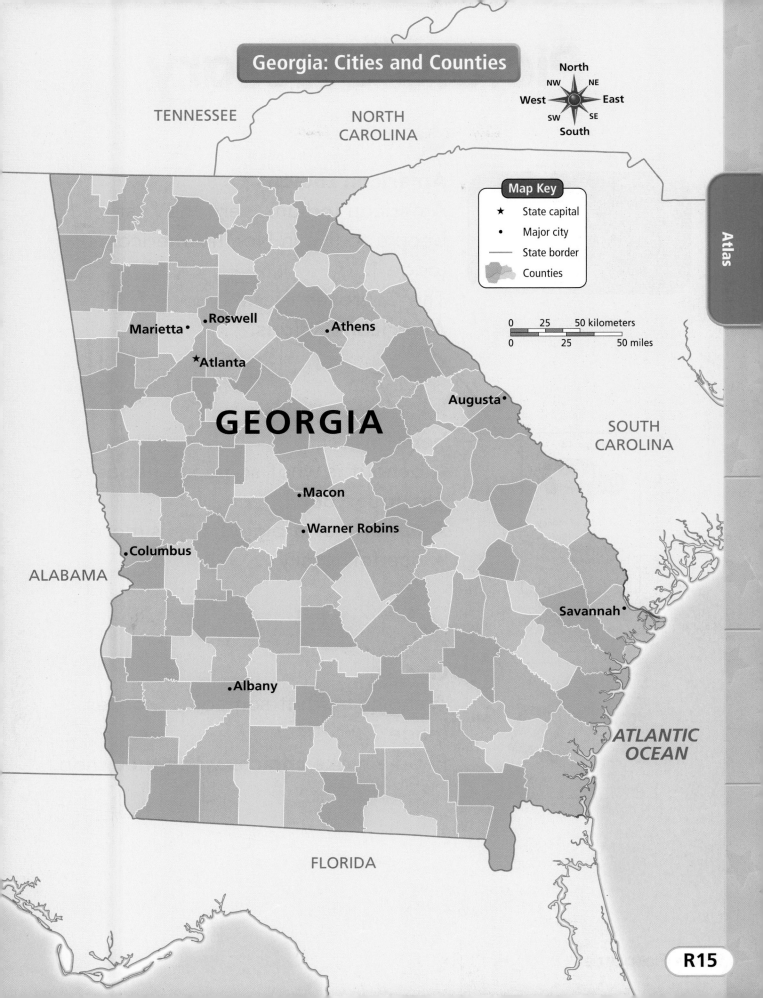

Picture Glossary

American Indians

American Indians were the first people to live in North America. (page 123)
The Cherokee is one group of **American Indians.**

benefit

Bigger Car

Cost: Lots of money

Benefit: More room for the family

A benefit is what someone hopes to get. (page 86)
A **benefit** of a bigger car is more space for family.

choice

$1.00

My First Year

$2.00

A choice is what someone chooses. (page 72)
People make **choices** when they shop.

citizen

A citizen is a person who belongs to a place. (page 39)
You are a **citizen** of the country where you live.

city

A city is a place where many people live close to one another. (page 40)
A **city** can have many tall buildings.

ATLANTIC
OCEAN

coast

A coast is land next to the ocean. (page 32)
The **coast** of Georgia is on the Atlantic Ocean.

communicate

When people share news and ideas, they communicate. (page 142)
We can **communicate** with children from other parts of the country.

communication

The way people share news and ideas is communication. (page 142)
Sign language is one kind of **communication.**

community

A community is a place where people live and work together. (page 80)
A town is a **community** that has homes, stores, and schools.

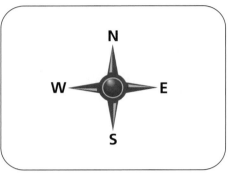

compass rose

A compass rose is a symbol that shows directions such as north, south, east, and west. (page 102)
A **compass rose** helps people find places on a map.

consumer

A consumer is someone who buys or uses goods or services. (page 90)
Many **consumers** buy food in stores near their homes.

continent

A continent is a very large area of land. (page 32)
North America is the **continent** where we live.

cost

The cost is what someone gives up to buy or get something. (page 84)
What is the **cost** of a pencil?

country

A country is land where people live under one government. (page 38)
The United States is the **country** where you live.

county

A county is a smaller part of a state. (page 39)
Georgia has 159 **counties.**

D

desert

A desert is a dry area that may sometimes be very hot. (page 41)
Plants that need little water grow in **deserts.**

election

An election is a time when citizens vote. (page 171)

In an **election,** people can vote for government leaders.

explorer

An explorer is someone who looks for places or things that are new to him or her. (page 126)

Lewis and Clark were **explorers** of land west of the Mississippi River.

fact

A fact is something that is true. (page 140)

It is a **fact** that Theodore Roosevelt was President of the United States.

factory

A factory is a place where workers use machines to make goods. (page 92)

Orange juice is made in a **factory.**

future
The future is time after today.
(page 116)
Tomorrow, next week, and next year
are all time in the **future.**

globe
A globe is a model of Earth. (page 30)
The **globe** shows Earth's continents
and oceans.

goods
Goods are things we buy or use.
(page 79)
A bakery sells **goods** such as rolls
and breads.

government
Government is the group of people
who run a community, county, state,
or country. (page 157)
People who work in **government**
work for all the citizens.

governor

A governor is the leader of state government. (page 164)
Who is the **governor** of your state?

hero

A hero is a person who does something brave or who works hard to help others. (page 24)
Harriet Tubman was a **hero** who led people to freedom.

history

History is the story of what happened in the past. (page 115)
When we read **history,** we learn about people who lived long ago.

honor

Honor means to show that someone or something is important to us. (page 176)
We **honor** our country when we say the "Pledge of Allegiance."

intermediate directions

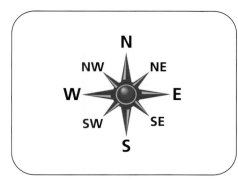

Intermediate directions are the directions between north, south, east, and west. (page 104)
Northwest and southwest are **intermediate directions.**

invention

An invention is a new tool or new way of doing something. (page 135)
The car was a great **invention.**

landform

Landforms are different shapes of land. (page 44)
Plains and mountains are both **landforms.**

law

A law is a community rule. (page 156)
It is a **law** that cars must stop at a stop sign.

Picture Glossary

machine

A machine is an object that does work for people. (page 98)
A **machine** can sort raisins.

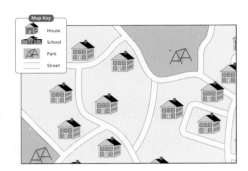

map

A map is a drawing of a place that shows a view from above. (page 36)
The **map** shows where the park is.

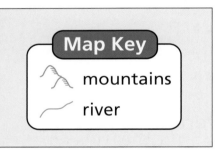

map key

The map key is the set of symbols found on a map. (page 36)
This **map key** shows two symbols.

mayor

A mayor is the leader of a city or town government. (page 164)
The **mayor** visited our school.

mountain

A mountain is land that is higher than all the land around it. (page 44) Mt. McKinley is the highest **mountain** in our country.

nation

A nation is a land with the same laws and leaders. (page 38) The United States of America is a **nation.**

natural resource

A natural resource is something in nature that people use. (page 50) Water is a very important **natural resource** for our lives.

needs

Needs are the things people must have to live. (page 70) Homes are **needs** for all people.

Pacific Ocean

ocean
An ocean is a large body of salty water. (page 31)
The Pacific **Ocean** is the world's largest ocean.

opinion
An opinion is what someone thinks about something. (page 140)
Two people may have different **opinions.**

past
The past is the time that happened before today. (page 114)
In the **past,** you were a baby.

plain
A plain is a large, flat land area. (page 44)
A **plain** can be grassy.

plateau

A plateau is a landform that is higher than the land around it. (page 47)
People climb up to a **plateau.**

present

The present is the time that is happening today. (page 114)
In the **present,** you are in first grade.

President

The President is the leader of the United States government. (page 165)
George Washington was the first **President** of our country.

primary source

A primary source is writing or telling about an event by someone who was there. (page 132)
Books that explorers wrote about what they saw are **primary sources.**

producer

A producer is someone who makes goods or gives services. (page 90)
People who work in factories are **producers.**

responsibility
A responsibility is a duty to do something. (page 169)
One **responsibility** a citizen has is to obey laws.

right
Something you are free to do is called a right. (page 168)
Citizens of our country have the **right** to speak freely.

save
To save means to put away and keep. (page 87)
Many people **save** money in a bank.

scarcity
Scarcity is not having enough of something. (page 70)
The county had a **scarcity** of rain, and water in city wells was low.

season

A season is a time of year with its own weather. (page 57)
Winter is usually the coldest **season.**

secondary source

A secondary source is writing or telling about an event by someone who was not there. (page 132)
Words people write now about the Pilgrims are **secondary sources.**

sell

To sell means to give things for money. (page 78)
Farmers can **sell** the food they grow to people who live in cities.

seller

A seller is a person who has goods or services that others can buy. (page 98)
This **seller** has many pets for sale.

services

Jobs people do to help others are called services. (page 79)
A doctor gives many health **services.**

settler

A settler is someone who comes to live in a place that is new to him or her. (page 123)
The Pilgrims were **settlers** in Plymouth.

spend

When people pay money, they spend it. (page 84)
People **spend** money to buy goods.

Georgia

state

A state is part of a country. (page 38)
Georgia is a **state** in the United States.

symbol

A symbol is a picture, place, or thing that stands for something else. (page 174)
Uncle Sam is a **symbol** of our country.

timeline

A timeline shows when events happened. (page 120)
A **timeline** can show the big events in your life.

transportation

Ways to move people and things from place to place are called transportation. (page 134)
A train is one kind of **transportation.**

valley

A valley is low land between hills or mountains. (page 46)
Many kinds of trees grow well in a **valley.**

volunteer

A volunteer is someone who chooses to work for no money. (page 79)
Joan and Charles are **volunteers** who help paint houses.

vote

When you vote, you make a choice. (page 170)
When citizens are 18 years old, they can **vote** for government leaders.

wants

Wants are things people would like to have. (page 72)
Having many, many toys are **wants** a child might have.

weather

Weather is what the air outside is like. (page 56)
Clouds are part of **weather.**

Index

Page numbers with *m* after them refer to maps.

Index

Index

Acknowledgments

For each of the selections listed below, grateful acknowledgment is made for permission to excerpt and/or reprint original or copyrighted material, as follows:

Permissioned Material

Excerpt from *Rush Hour,* by Christine Loomis. Text copyright ©1996 by Christine Loomis. Reprinted by permission of Houghton Mifflin Company.

Illustrations

34–35 Michael Maydak 44, 45 Tracy Sabin 56, 78–79 Sally Vitsky 58–59 Mircea Catusanu 60 Alex Burnet 71, 160, 161, 184 Cheryl Mendenhall 74–75, 76, 77 Laurence Cleyet-Merle 92–93 Christiane Beauregard 94–95 Steve Costanza 118–119 Mark & Rosemary Jarman 120–121 Chris Lensch 123 Robert Van Nutt 142 Will Williams 187, 188–189, 196 Matt Archambault 187, 190–191, 192–193 Steve Harrington 187, 194–195 Craig Orback

Map Credits

Mapping Specialists, Ltd.
Maps.com
Ortelious Design

Photography

7 (b) ©HMCo./Ken Karp. 8 (b) Bridgeman Art Library. 9 (bl) Henry T. Kaiser/IndexStock Imagery. 10 (b) ©HMCo./Ken Karp. 14 (t) Courtesy of Georgia Department of Economic Development. 23 (bkgd) William Manning/CORBIS. 23 (bc) Photodisc Blue/Getty Images. 24 (bl) National Portrait Gallery, Smithsonian Institution/Art Resource, NY. (cl) Independence National Historical Park. (cr) Independence National Historical Park. (br) The Granger Collection, New York. 25 (bl) The Granger Collection, New York. (cl) © CORBIS. (br) Library of Congress, Prints & Photographs Division, [reproduction number, e.g., LC-J7-1234]. 26–27 (bkgd) Courtesy of Georgia Department of Economic Development. 28 (br) Jim Steinberg/Photo Researchers. 29 (l) ML Sinibaldi/CORBIS. (r) Phoebe Dunn/Stock Connection/PictureQuest. 30 (br) ©HMCo./Ken Karp. 33 (tl) Adalberto Rios Szalav/Sexto Sol/Photodisc/Getty Images. (tr) Photo 24/Brand X/Getty Images. 38 (b) ©HMCo./Ken Karp. 40 (bl) Pegaz/Alamy. (br) Bill Ross/CORBIS. 41 (t) Lonely Planet Images 2000. 44–45 (b) Frank Staub/Index Stock Imagery/PictureQuest. 45 (c) MacDuff Everton/CORBIS. 46 (b) James Randklev Photography. (cr) Elk Photography. 48–49 (bkgd) Courtesy of Georgia Department of Economic Development. 50 (br) Royalty-Free/CORBIS. 51 (t) J.A. Kraulis/Masterfile. (cl) Tom Algire/SuperStock. (cr) W. Cody/CORBIS. 52 (tr) Peter Christopher/Masterfile. (b) Arthur Tilley/i2i Images/PictureQuest. 53 (c) Craig Hammell/CORBIS. 54 (tl) CORBIS. (b) Theodore Roosevelt Collection, Harvard College Library (bMS Am 1541 (288, no. 3). Permission granted by the Houghton Library, Harvard University and The Theodore Roosevelt Association. 55 (bl) National Portrait Gallery, Smithsonian Institution/Art Resource, NY. 57 (tl) Dennis Lane/Index Stock Imagery. (tr) Richard Hutchings/Photo Edit. (bl) Peter Christopher/Masterfile. (br) Bill Bachmann/Photo Edit. 58 (tr) Rommel/Masterfile. (br) Greg Scott/Masterfile. 59 (cl) Rommel/Masterfile. (tr) Rubberball. 61 (b) ©HMCo./Morocco Flowers. 65 (bl) National Portrait Gallery, Smithsonian Institution/Art Resource, NY. 66–67 (bkgd) Palmer Kane Studios. 68 (cr) Lawrence Migdale/Stone/Getty Images. 69 (cr) Diaphor Agency/Index Stock Imagery. 70 (br) ©HMCo./Ken Karp. 72 (t) Wonderfile/Masterfile. (c) Photodisc/Punch-Stock. (b) C Squared Studios/Photodisc/

Getty Images. 73 (c) ©HMCo./Ken Karp. (tr) C Squared Studios/Photodisc/Getty Images. (cr) Photodisc/Punch-Stock. 80 (bl) Charles Gupton/CORBIS. (br) Michael Newman/Photo Edit. 81 (tr) Royalty-Free/CORBIS. (cl) Kevin Dodge/Masterfile. 82 (c) Rosemary Cloud, City of East Point Fire Department. 82–83 (bkgd) SuperStock/PictureQuest. 85 (b) ©HMCo./Ken Karp. 86 (cl) Kerrick James Photography/Stone/Getty Images. (cr) Hal Lott/CORBIS. (br) Ariel Skelley/Masterfile. 87 (c) Silver Editions. 88 (t) ©HMCo./Ken Karp. (c) ©HMCo./Ken Karp. (b) ©HMCo./Ken Karp. 89 (bkgd) ©HMCo./Ken Karp. 90 (b) Creasource/Series/PictureQuest. 91 (tl) CORBIS. (cl) Photodisc/Getty Images. (bl) Felicia Martinez/Photo Edit. (tr) Spencer Grant/Photo Edit. (cr) HIRB/Index Stock Imagery. (br) Fabrik Studios/Index Stock Imagery. (c) Comstock/PunchStock. 92 (br) Wonderfile. 94 (cl) Sheila Rock/EMI Classics/ICM Artists Ltd. 95 (l) Courtesy of Maria and Fernando Bujones. 96–97 (c) Photodisc Collection/Getty Images. 98 (bl) Steve Vidler/SuperStock. (br) Richard T. Nowitz/CORBIS. 99 (tl) Dynamic Graphics/Creatas. (tr) ©HMCo./Ken Karp. 100 (bc) Jane Grushow/Grant Heilman Photography—All Rights Reserved. (br) ©#797998 Index Stock Imagery, Inc. (cl) Library of Congress, Prints & Photographs Division, [reproduction number, e.g., LC-J7-1234]. 101 (t) Bettmann/CORBIS. 109 (b) Stock Montage, Getty Images. 110–111 (bkgd) Palmer Kane Studios. 112 (cl) CORBIS. (br) Rick Egan. 113 (cl) Premium Stock/CORBIS. (cr) Rob & Sas/CORBIS. 114 (br) Chris Windsor/Photodisc/Getty Images. (r) Photo Link/Photodisc/PictureQuest. 115 (t) The Image Bank/Getty Images. (c) The Image Bank/Getty Images. (b) Norbert Schaefer/CORBIS. 116 (tc) Scott Vincent. (cr) Nancy Brown/Getty Images. 117 (tl) Digital Vision/Getty Images. (cl) Bruce Coleman. 118–119 (c) ©HMCo./Ken Karp. 122 (b) Bettmann/CORBIS. 126 (b) Rick Egan. 127 (c) The Granger Collection, New York. 128 (br) The Granger Collection, New York. (bl) Independence National Historical Park. 129 (bl) The Granger Collection, New York. 130 (bl) The United States Mint. 131 (c) The Granger Collection, New York. (bl) Montana Historical Society. 134 (b) Bridgeman Art Library. 135 (c) Bettmann/CORBIS. 136 (tl) CORBIS. (tr) Charles Benes/Index Stock Imagery. 137 (tl) Tom Brakefield/CORBIS. (tr) Stone/Getty Images. 138–139 (bkgd) Roy Ooms/Masterfile. 141 (br) Bettmann/CORBIS. (bl) George H. H. Huey/CORBIS. 143 (r) Jacqui Hurst/CORBIS. 144 (b) ©HMCo./Comstock. (tr) Davies + Starr/Imagebank/Getty Images. (cl) Underwood & Underwood/CORBIS. 145 (tr) Guy Grenier/Masterfile. (tc) Tom Wagner/CORBIS. (tl) NASA. 146 (tl) National Portrait Gallery, Smithsonian Institution/Art Resource, NY. 147 (t) The Granger Collection, New York. (bl) The Corcoran Gallery of Art/CORBIS. 151 (bl) Montana Historical Society. (b) The Corcoran Gallery of Art/CORBIS. 152–153 (bkgd) Jerry Tobias/CORBIS. 154 (cl) Courtesy of the City of Atlanta Mayor's Office. (cr) Independence National Historical Park. 155 (cl) Andy Sacks/Stone/Getty Images. (cr) CORBIS. 157 (c) David Young-Wolff/Photo Edit. 159 (t) ©HMCo./Carol Kaplan Photography. (c) Photodisc/Getty Images. (bl) ©HMCo./Carol Kaplan Photography. 163 (t) Jeff Greenberg's Collection/Index Stock Imagery. (c) Joe Sohm/The Image Works. (b) Miles Ertman/Masterfile. 164 (br) AP World Wide Photo. (cl) Courtesy of the City of Atlanta Mayor's Office. 165 (tr) Reuters New Media Inc. 166 (tl) Independence National Historical Park. (b) Photodisc/Getty Images (digital composite). 167 (t) SuperStock. (bl) Independence National Historical Park. 168 (b) ©HMCo./

Jade Albert. 169 (tl) The Greater Boston Food Bank. (cr) The Greater Boston Food Bank. (b) ©HMCo./Ken Karp. 172 (tl) CORBIS. 173 (t) "Harriet Tubman" by Jane DeDecker, National Sculptors' Guild. (bl) CORBIS. 174 (b) Burke/Triolo/Brand X Pictures/Getty Images. 175 (r) James Lafayette/Index Stock Imagery. 176 (bl) Henryk T. Kaiser/Index Stock Imagery. 177 (t) Jeff Vanuga/CORBIS. 178 (tr) Hillary Wilkes/International Stock. 179 (tr) CORBIS. 180 (br) Tony Freeman/Photo Edit. 181 (bkgd) Bettmann/CORBIS. 182 (tl) Richard Hutchings/Photo Edit. (tr) David Young-Wolff/Photo Edit. 185 (bc) Independence National Historical Park. (br) CORBIS. 186 ©HMCo./Ken Karp. 199 ©HMCo./Ken Karp. R1 (c) Bruce Burkhardt/CORBIS. R2 (b) Paul Fusco/Magnum Photos. R3 (t) Jerry Tobias/CORBIS. R4 (cl) Bettmann/CORBIS. (br) CORBIS. R6 (tl) Art Wolfe/Stone/Getty Images. (tr) Michael T. Sedam/CORBIS. R7 (tl) Orion Press/Stone/Getty Images. (br) D. Rose/Zefa/Masterfile. R16 (tl) Kevin Fleming/CORBIS. (cl) Hal Lott/CORBIS. (bl) Photodisc/Punch-Stock. (b) C Squared Studios/Photodisc/Getty Images. R17 (t) Ariel Skelley/Masterfile. (tl) Andrew Gordon/2003 Panoramic Images. (bl) Jose Luis Pelaez, Inc./CORBIS. (b) Jeff Greenberg/Photo Edit. R18 (tl) Dennis O'Clair/Stone/Getty Images. (cl) ©HMCo./Ken Karp. R19 (tl) ©HMCo./Ken Karp. (bl) Lonely Planet Images 2000. R20 (tl) Andy Sacks/Stone/Getty Images. (cl) The Granger Collection, New York. (bl) Dynamic Graphics/Creatas. R21 (cl) ©HMCo./Ken Karp. (bl) Wonderfile. (b) Ghislain & Marie David de Lossy/The Image Bank/Getty Images. R22 (tl) AP World Wide Photo. (cl) CORBIS. (bl) Kevin Fleming/CORBIS. (b) Bruce Burkhardt/CORBIS. R23 (cl) Underwood & Underwood/CORBIS. (bl) Jim Steinberg/Photo Researchers. R24 (tl) JP Maroot. (bl) Courtesy of the City of Atlanta Mayor's Office. R25 (tl) Frank Staub/Index Stock Imagery/PictureQuest. (cl) Royalty-Free/CORBIS. (bl) Charles Register/Picturesque/PictureQuest. R26 (tl) Image produced by F. Hasler, M. Jentoft-Nilsen, H. Pierce, K. Palaniappan, and M. Manyin. NASA Goddard Lab for Atmospheres—data from National Oceanic and Atmospheric Administration/NASA. (bl) Nancy Brown/Getty Images. (b) Mark Heifner/Pan Stock/PictureQuest. R27 (t) Elk Photography. (tl) Arthur Tilley/Taxi/Getty Images. (cl) Bettmann/CORBIS. (bl) The Granger Collection, New York. (b) Ed Lallo/Index Stock Imagery. R28 (tl) Stone/Getty Images. (cl) ©HMCo./Angela Coppola. (bl) ©HMCo./Ken Karp. (b) Royalty-Free/CORBIS. R29 (tl) Bill Bachmann/Photo Edit. (cl) Rachel Epstein/Photo Edit. (b) Micael Newman/Photo Edit. (b) Royalty-Free/CORBIS. R30 (tr) Nik Wheeler/CORBIS. (cl) ©HMCo./Ken Karp. (bl) Thinkstock/Getty Images. R31 (tl) Jerome Tisne/Taxi/Getty Images. (tc) John Henley/CORBIS. (cl) Premium Stock/CORBIS. (bl) James Randklev Photography. (b) Richard Steinmetz. R32 (tl) Richard Hutchings/Photo Edit. (cl) Palmer Kane Studios. (bl) Mark L. Stephenson/CORBIS.

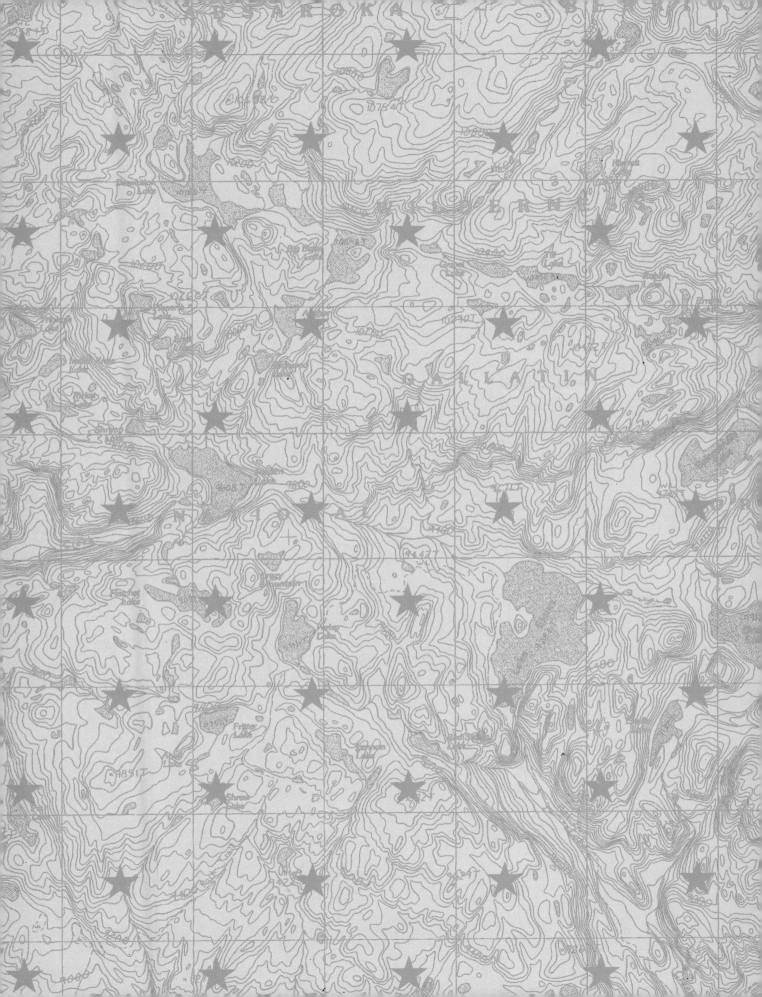

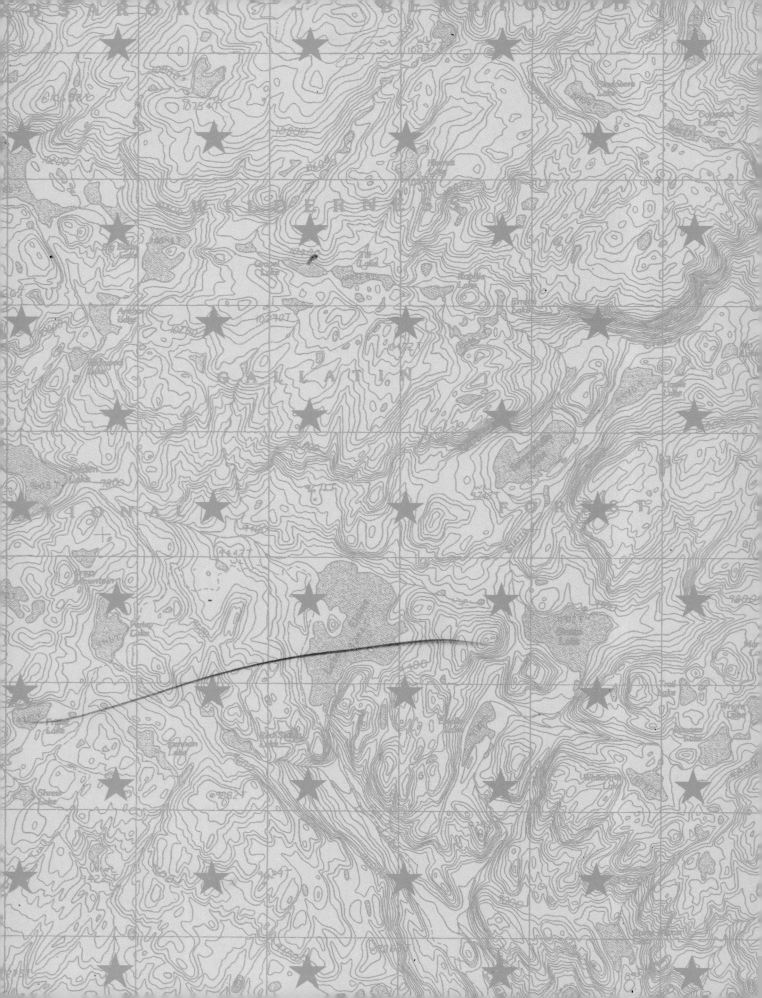